To Tom and Marcia
best wishes to antique lovers
Peg Weymer

Threads of Tradition
Northwest Pennsylvania
Quilts

Edited by Marianne Berger Woods

Crawford County Historical Society
Meadville, Pennsylvania
1997

COVER ILLUSTRATION

Pineapple Quilt by Lottie Estella Polley Young, c. 1910,
owned by Evelyn Grabigel (see page 51),
photo by Bob Lowry

PUBLICATION ACKNOWLEDGEMENTS

Photography by Bob Lowry
Chapter illustrations by Carol Kennemuth
Copy-editing by E. B. Green Editorial
Publication design by Jonathan Miller
Printing by Commercial Printing, New Castle, Pennsylvania

EXHIBITION ACKNOWLEDGEMENTS

Andrew Chakalis, *Exhibition Designer*
Karen March, *Exhibition Consultant*
Jennifer Lapham, *Visiting Director, Allegheny College Galleries*
Robert Raczka, *Director, Allegheny College Galleries*
John Vanco, *Director, Erie Art Museum*
Suzanne Adham and Ruth Pierson, *Education and Docent Coordinators*

Bowman, Penelec, and Megahan Galleries, Allegheny College
Meadville, Pennsylvania
9 September–8 October
1997

Erie Art Museum
Erie, Pennsylvania
11 October–17 December
1997

To Peg

*I*t was not a woman's desire. . .

to be forgotten. And in one

simple, unpretentious way, she

created a medium that would

outlive even many of her

husband's houses, barns and

fences; she signed her name in

friendship onto cloth and, in

her own way, cried out,

Remember me.

—LINDA OTTO LIPSETT,
Remember Me: Women and Their Friendship Quilts

Donors

DEDICATIONS

To an **anonymous donor** *providing funds for copies of*
Threads of Tradition *to be distributed to libraries in the seven counties*

•

In loving memory of **Lucile Richard Pierson,**
a tribute by her son and his wife, Richard & Ruth Pierson

In loving memory of **Margaret B. & Timothy F. Gorman**
by their son, William F. Gorman

To **Ethel Moore Miller** *from Franklin & Dorothy Miller*

In memory of their mother, **Berneice Haight Patterson,**
a skilled quilter for over sixty years and the keeper of their quilt heritage,
by Mary Beth Patterson Hagamen and David Patterson

In loving Memory of **Paul V. Kebert** *by his wife Pauline E. Kebert*

In honor of Walter's grandmother, **Mary Margaret Mosbacher Jehn,**
by Walter & Elizabeth Greenleaf

In loving memory of my mother, **Margaret Shontz Todd,**
who kept the tradition of quilting alive in my family,
by her daughter, Joyce Todd Ladner

In loving memory of her mother, **Minnie Rapp McKnight,**
who passed on her heritage and love of home-related arts to her three daughters,
by Peg Weymer

PATRONS

Janice Horn • Christine B. & Richard A. Lang • Louise and John Mangus
Sally & Wayne Merrick • Marianne Berger Woods

SPONSORS

Christine & Jack Bailey • Miriam Bowman • Linda & Bill DeArment • Gail & Ed Fine
Doris R. & John K. Foster • Frances & Paul Huber • Vivian & Michael Hyde
June & Dick Kleeman • Gail McClure, The Quilt Square • B. Ann & Chester Phelps
Betty & Fran Richmond • Elissa M. Stuttler • William Witherup

Contents

Preface

*P*erhaps the recognition in the mid-1970s of quilts as objects of art and quiltmakers as artists concomitant with scholarship into the lives and works of women artists in America was more than coincidental. The decade of the 1960s, leading to this flowering of interest in historical women, had been tumultuous. The unequal treatment of women and African Americans caught the attention of the masses, and they joined forces in protestation. (Feminists and abolitionists had united in the antebellum era as well).

While the outward expression of frustration with inequality in the United States came through demonstrations, riots, and reported bra-burnings, a quieter and more reflective movement was taking place. Students and scholars were perusing diaries, dusty library shelves, un-indexed texts, attics, and trunks to locate information about women. Their findings emerged for public dissemination in the next decade with Patsy and Myron Orlofsky's *Quilts in America,* published in 1974, and *Women Artists: 1550–1950,* co-curated by Linda Nochlin and Ann Sutherland Harris in 1976. Both *Quilts in America* and the landmark exhibition and exhibition catalog *Women Artists* brought to the fore women who earlier had received only the most brief mention, if any, in *his*tory books.

Before the mid-seventies, at least one quilt text was written each decade: *The Romance of the Patchwork Quilt* by Carrie A. Hall and Rose G. Kretsinger in 1935, *American Quilts and Coverlets* by Florence Peto in 1949, *Patchwork* by Averil Colby in 1958 and *The Standard Book of Quilt-Making and Collecting* by Marguerite Ickis in 1959, *Historical Needlework of Pennsylvania* by Margaret B. Schiffer in 1968, and *Quilts and Coverlets* by Jean Ray Laury and *Old Patchwork Quilts and the Women Who Made Them* by Ruth Finley in the early 1970s.

The 1980s were rich in the documentation and exhibition of quilts, beginning with the Kentucky Quilt Project, Inc., in 1981. State, county, and local quilt documentation projects popped up like crocuses on a warm spring day, and the work has continued in the last decade of the century. *Gatherings: America's Quilt Heritage* by Kathlyn F. Sullivan (exhibition curated by Paul D. Pilgrim and Gerald E. Roy) chronicled the national events that took place before 1995. In and through such quilt documentation, people have found a vehicle to eradicate the slight befallen to women's history—especially of local women's history.

This particular undertaking, originally called the "Northwest Pennsylvania Quilt Documentation Project," was the dream of quilt historian/designer/restoration specialist Peg Weymer. When Peg, learned that, after directing a similar project in northwestern Arkansas, I had moved back to Meadville in 1987, she thought she had a co-conspirator. I wasn't so sure, especially when we could not at first find a sponsoring agency or obtain grant money. A cadre of Meadville folks was willing, but we weren't sure about help from the other six counties. But Peg persisted, even through my teaching at an out-of-state-college, finally interesting former curator of the Crawford County Historical Society (CCHS) Leslie Przybylek and librarian at Clarion University of Pennsylvania Janice Horn, and recruiting design specialist Vivian Hyde to help with organization and fund-raising. In the fall of 1995 Peg called and Vivian led a meeting at the Market House in Meadville, which women from almost every county attended. This time we were off and running!

During the period before this meeting, several groups invited three quilt experts to Meadville to "fire us up." In 1987 Libby Carlisle arranged for Patsy Orlofsky to survey the quilts at the Crawford County Historical Society's historic Baldwin-Reynolds House. With a technical assistance grant from the Pennsylvania Historical and Museums Commission, she taught area residents the "dos and don'ts" of caring for quilts and the best methods of restoring them. In 1990, through the generosity of a Pennsylvania Humanities Council (PHC) "Commonwealth Speakers" grant, Yvonne Milspaw came to speak at the Market House. She taught us the importance of the quiltmakers' stories and how they relate to the larger picture of American history. Then we secured Ohio quilt historian Ricky Clark, who spoke to the issue of documentation and "how-to-do-it" one frigid day in March 1994, at the Baldwin-Reynolds House. That seminar was funded by the Meadville Antique Study Club and The Antiquarians.

Meanwhile in Erie County, Susan Beates Hansen, director of interpretation at the Erie County Historical Society, engaged a panel of experts for the Battles Museum Fifth Annual Conference on Rural Life: Quilts and Coverlets in May 1992. The conference was funded in part through a grant from the PHC. Joining Hansen, who presented quilts from Erie County, were material culture specialist Jeannette Lasansky, textile historian Virginia Gunn, and costume historian Mary-Ellen Perry.

In early 1996 we received a grant from the Quilter's Guild of Dallas as seed money for the documentation phase of the project, Phase I. Whether that generosity may be attributed to southern hospitality, the American spirit of quiltmaking, or simply our need, the fact remains that the guild helped us when we *really* needed help. Marian Ann Montgomery and Frances Hafer were the guild's co-chairs at the time of the grant.

Carol Kennemuth and Janice Horn of Clarion County designed and quilted a "fund-raising" quilt (page x), won by Laurel Swartz of Erie. We made more than two thousand dollars with that quilt, but there were other fund-raising efforts as well. June Kleeman designed a project (tree) logo, and we sold logo pins; she and a group of quiltmakers organized a quilt show at the Unitarian Church in Meadville; the Meadville Antique Study Club gave us seed money of five hundred dollars; we organized a fund drive; we are selling a *Threads of Tradition* signed and numbered print—an original design by Mary Hamilton; and we had two fabric sales that netted more than two thousand dollars. The Franklin sale was organized by Rainy Linn, and Carol Kennemuth organized the Shannondale sale. We received donations of fabrics, books, quilting notions and patterns, and batting from many commercial vendors. Countryside Quilts and Country Bear Creations, both in Clarion County, also contributed to the sales. In addition, Peg Weymer's sister Rebecca McKnight Till donated feedsacks and yards of fabric.

We received a generous $26,000 gift-and-matching grant from the Pennsylvania Humanities Council to fund the traveling exhibition. Matching money has come from the Meadville Antique Study Club, an area foundation that wishes to remain anonymous, and Sanray Corporation.

We are grateful to all those mentioned and others not mentioned for their support. To those who bought a roll of batting or paid five dollars for one of our pins—it meant a lot to us!

But I must not leave you with the notion that my skepticism about the project persisted. I enjoy writing—even doing grant proposals—and I like research even more. Once the quilts were chosen and I was able to delve into the lives of the women (and men) who carefully, tediously, and lovingly cut, arranged, juxtaposed, and stitched the fabrics, I was in my element. While we don't know their average age at death, almost every quiltmaker seems to have been blessed with longevity. I will probably never see a quilt without the image of Maude Briggs Zahner (page 36) coming to mind. There is something to be said for the old saying, "Busy hands are happy hands." I know mine have been busy since this project got rolling.

All of the stories included about the quiltmakers here were read by the owner/s of each quilt before publication. She/he/they made comments/corrections and returned the essays in the kind of interactive research and writing that I believe is critical to integrating object and subject. The quilt owners have been cooperative and helpful in every respect. After the quilts were chosen, for example,

Northwest Pennsylvania Pines
1996
98" x 92"
Carol Kennemuth and Janice Horn

we had little time to gather them up for the photography session scheduled in Erie in early May. Everyone worked together to make it happen. The chairwomen from each county did an exceptional job as well. Again, thank you!

As for the book before you, we have been able to put that together, too, in what seemed too little time—again through the cooperation of quilt owners, committee, and essayists. Together the documentors and owners assigned a name to each of the quilts, however nondefinitive. (The same styles have different name in different areas of the United States.) We would have preferred to use each quiltmaker's own name for her/his quilt, but in most cases the name was not handed down with the quilt.

Neither would we have had a catalog without the support of the CCHS, which came through after we learned that the PHC does not, as a matter of policy, fund anything requiring purchase by the general public. I had come to grips with that and thought everyone on our committee had, too. But, at the March meeting, when I showed the kind of brochure that PHC funds would support, Carol Kennemuth's mouth dropped: "Then we can't have a book?" "No, we can't," I replied. Carol's sad face told me we had to do it. The Crawford County Historical Society stepped forward, and we hurried. We hope you enjoy the result.

The project was divided into two time-and-task segments that we identified as Phase I and Phase II. Phase I, focusing on documentation, began in the fall of 1995 and ended a year later. Each county held at least one "Quilt Discovery Day" during which quilts were brought to be registered and photographed. The Phase I committee consisted of these women:

Jane Clark	Carol Kennemuth	Mary Schliecker
Susan Beates Hansen	Rainy Linn	Edith Serkownek
Nancy Heath	Christine Mitchell	Phyllis Weltner
Gladys Herrick	Ruth Prest	Peg Weymer
Janice Horn	Leslie Przybylek	Marianne Berger Woods
Vivian Hyde	Calla Joy Rose	

Phase II began with the task of choosing just forty-six from the more than a thousand documented quilts made before 1940. The responsibilities of the Phase II committee included the implementation of the PHC grant and the preparation and publication of *Threads of Tradition: Northwest Pennsylvania Quilts*. The committee included:

Jane Clark	Vivian Hyde	Edith Serkownek
Ruth Cummings	Carol Kennemuth	Peg Weymer
Betty Fortenier	Rainy Linn	Marianne Berger Woods,
Janice Horn	Vivian Moon	*ex-officio*

Thanks again to the Crawford County Historical Society for its continued support, and especially to John Petruso for his many signatures and meetings and for leading the pack (his board) to rally behind us! Thanks also to Kenneth Montag for his accounting and for signing the checks!

— MARIANNE BERGER WOODS

Project Director

Clarion County

Nestled among lushly wooded hills, and situated alongside the river that eventually gave the area its name, is Clarion County. Originally used as hunting ground by the Seneca Indians, this territory was claimed in 1753 by the French, who stayed mainly in Venango County, never venturing beyond their garrison. More concerned with keeping their fort at Niagara during the French-Indian War, they abandoned it in 1759.

Christian Frederick Post thus was the first white man known to set foot in Clarion County. The Prosperity Council sent him to the area with a message for the tribes living on the Allegheny River in hopes of winning them over to the English during the French-Indian War. During his travels, Post happened through the northern part of the county. His was to be the last white face for some time, for after the French left the area, it remained a hunting ground for the Seneca as well as for neighboring tribes.

In 1784 the Seneca and the chiefs of the Six Nations signed a deed granting to the government all the land remaining in what is now the northern and northwestern part of the state. Starting in 1785 many people bought land in the area, but not until about 1792 did anyone take permanent residence in the county. Then Absalom Travis and his sons settled on land in the southeast corner of Monroe Township. Travis died around 1795, others—sturdy, hardworking, pious and steadfast churchgoers—endured.

Clarion County was formally created in 1839, when Governor David Porter signed an act granting its organization. Farming was the main occupation for many years, but abundant mineral wealth, along with the vast forested tracts of the region, soon brought other industries to the area. From mid- to late-nineteenth century, Clarion County saw the rise and fall of the iron industry, the oil speculation craze, and the lumber industry, as well as of coal mining.

Throughout this time, women worked alongside their husbands, helping to build their homes and secure a future for their families. They had little time for social activities other than helping their neighbors with house- or barn-raisings. In the late 1800s, women still lived at home on the farm, leaving only to marry and work alongside their farmer husbands to create homes of their own. Education was limited to the early grades, when children attended school at all.

As the new century dawned, women began to further their education, some graduating from high school and continuing on to college, becoming teachers and working in the one-room schools populating the area. Other women started their own businesses, and a few even worked with husbands in their offices. But many women continued to marry and raise families while working on farms. Social life still revolved mainly around the church and its related activities, but women also formed and belonged to social organizations.

The Great Depression of the 1930s was barely felt by most people in this county; as self-sufficient farmers they were able to grow almost everything they needed to survive. Many merchants managed to survive as well, even while extending credit to those unable to pay.

Piecing and quilting were squeezed into the time between the myriad tasks comprising "women's work." The *Clarion Republican* announced a quilt exhibit April 21–22, 1933, at the Parish House of the Baptist Church in Clarion. "Quilt lovers" were invited to come and bring their quilts. It cost ten cents to enter a quilt and if the quilt was sold, 10 percent of the sale price went to the church. Three prizes were awarded by popular vote. Exhibitions and competitions such as this were likely to inspire Clarion County women to pay particular attention to doing their best.

By the end of the 1930s Clarion County had survived the Great Depression, thanks to the hardiness and spirit of the descendants of those early pioneers who chose to carve out a new life for themselves in the wilderness more than two hundred years earlier.

— MARY CARTER-JOHNSON

Sara Quilt
c. 1800–1825
42½ x 28 inches
Phillips Family Member

A VERY SMALL CRIB QUILT WAS MADE DURING THE FIRST QUARTER OF THE NINETEENTH century for someone named Sara in the Phillips family from Clarion. Although in quilt lingo it would be called a Nine Patch Variation, it is more commonly known as the Sara Quilt because it has been passed down to subsequent family members named Sara. In generations without a Sara, the quilt resided with another member of the family. Now in the care of Mona and Louraine Smith, it awaits the time when their granddaughter Jill Sara Rapp is old enough to appreciate her family heirloom and take responsibility for keeping the Phillips legacy alive. The quilt was given to Mona for safekeeping by the last Sara to have had "official custody," Jill Sara's great-grandmother, Sara Phillips Smith. Sara was known to her twin great-granddaughters (Joy Mary is Jill Sara's sister) as Grandma Sally, and they have fond memories of the tea parties they shared with her before her death in 1995.

Turkey Tracks
c. 1869
106 x 96 inches
Bridget Hayes Slattery
(1840–1924)

CRATES (FORMERLY RED BANK) IS A LONG WAY FROM IRELAND WHERE BRIDGET HAYES WAS born in 1840. At age twelve she emigrated to Champlain Village, New York, with her parents, but when they died she moved to Pittsburgh to live with a sister. There they were both professional seamstresses. Bridget married Patrick Slattery on November 27, 1865, and the couple moved to Limestone. In 1900 they left to make their final home in Crates. Bridget made her pretty Turkey Tracks quilt several years after she was married – perhaps while she awaited the birth of her first child, Dennis, in 1869. Another son and four daughters – three of whom were named Mary after Bridget's mother – followed. Though Bridget was busy rearing her family, this quilt is likely not the only one she made. She died in 1924. Catherine D. Shannon now owns the quilt.

Bridget Hayes Slattery

Flying Geese
c. 1870
84 x 80 inches
Mary Elizabeth
Reynolds Coates
(1828–1903)

A FLYING GEESE QUILT, MADE BY MARY ELIZABETH REYNOLDS COATES IN THE 1870S, HASN'T flown far. Mary Elizabeth was born in Hartford County, Maryland, where at age thirty-four she married on Christmas Day 1862. She and her husband, Samuel A. Coates, later moved to Fern, Pennsylvania. After moving to Clarion County, Sam and their eldest son, Rolland, began working in the oil fields in the Fern and Cogley area. The Coateses eventually found oil on their forty-four-acre farm and produced their own premium-grade oil. During the years of the oil boom, Fern was said to be "one of the wickedest towns ever built!" Mary Elizabeth died at age seventy-five in 1903. Sam died four years later at age seventy-eight. Their graves remained unmarked until 1987 when their grandson, William A. M. Coates, then eighty-seven, had a tombstone erected on the spot he remembered as their burial place from when he attended their funerals at age seven and eleven. M. Gene and Marian Hummel Master now own this quilt.

Mary Elizabeth Reynolds Coates

Mary Caroline Basim Ion's sixtieth birthday party at The Old Brick House, 1891

Mary Caroline Basim Ion (detail from above)

A CRIB QUILT WAS MADE C. 1872 FOR BIRD SHELDON ION BY HIS MOTHER, MARY CAROLINE Basim Ion. Both Mary and her husband, Richard Redfore Ion, were of English heritage and were born in Clarion County. Richard's parents, John and Margaret Ion, emigrated to America in 1818–19 (he came first and she followed with three children). After living awhile in a log home, they built a fine brick mansion (above) and sent to England for their furnishings. The home still stands and was immortalized in a poem, "The Old Brick House," by Pearl Reinsel Ion, Bird's wife. Richard was born in 1824, possibly before the house was completed; Mary was born in 1830. They married in Strattanville in 1853 and subsequently became the parents of eight children. In 1873, son Bird Sheldon was born in the brick house. Whether Mary made a small quilt for each of the other seven is not known. But Bird treasured the Nine Patch Variation quilt she had made for him, and he gave it to his daughter, Regina Ion Sacolic, before he died in 1950. Regina was raised in the family home as were her children; thus five continuous generations have occupied "The Old Brick House."

Nine Patch Variation
1873
40 x 36 inches
Mary Caroline Basim Ion (1830–1908)

*Lydia C. Jones Master with her sisters
(Lydia is second from left)*

Ladies Aid Society, Trinity Evangelical Congregational Church

THE DRESDEN PLATE WAS A POPULAR PATTERN IN THE 1930S, BUT THE VARIATION KNOWN AS Dresden Fan was not. Lydia C. Jones Master went a step farther in originality, making both a Dresden Fan quilt and a matching pillow cover in 1930. This combination is rare; she likely found the pattern in a magazine. Lydia's obituary noted that she was "well known as a lover of flowers . . . [her garden was] one of the beauty spots of the community." Her quiltmaking, however, has provided her some semblance of immortality. Two of Lydia's many quilts are in the Collections of the Sandford Gallery at Clarion University of Pennsylvania. Whether her four sisters or mother quilted is uncertain, but daughter Mable Master Shorts did take up the art. Mable's Streak of Lightning quilt graces the gallery's "Manson Family Quilts Collection." Lydia was born on a farm at Jones Corner (near Emlenton) in 1857 and married William Allison (Al) Master of Fern on March 6, 1876. Al was a carpenter and "rig builder" during the 1880s oil boom. Shortly before 1900 the couple bought the Fern General Store and Post Office, which they operated until 1916. Lydia, no doubt exposed to the many new fabrics that came to the store, provided a colorful palette for her quilts. She made quilts for her four children and thirteen grandchildren, each one ready at the new child's birth. Lydia was a member of the Ladies Aid Society of the Trinity Evangelical Congregational Church in Fern for more than forty years. She died on March 1, 1939, her eighty-second birthday.

Dresden Fan Quilt and Pillow Cover
c. 1930
79½ x 78 inches
Lydia C. Jones Master (1857–1939)

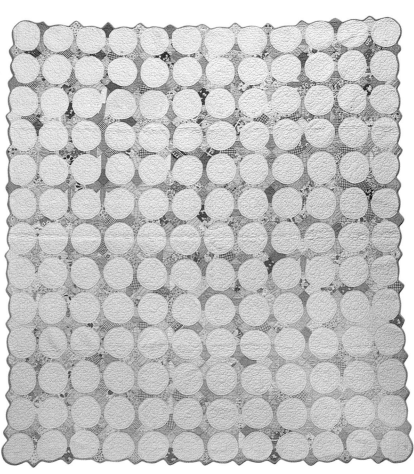

Virginia Snowball
c. 1930
68 x 76 inches
Ocie Bish Shoup
(1905–1970)

OCIE BISH WAS THE DAUGHTER OF THE FOUNDERS OF BISHTOWN. THE FAMILY ORIGINALLY emigrated to America from Holland, though both Ocie's parents, Adam Monroe and Carrie Viola Bish, were born in Bishtown, where they resided after their marriage and where Ocie was born. Ocie made this Virginia Snowball quilt c. 1930, after she married William Jacob Shoup, a German from New Bethlehem. They married in 1922 and later became the parents of a son and two daughters. Ocie's mother taught her to quilt; her expert stitching shows she learned very well. Ocie also liked to crochet. Carolyn Matthews Miller now owns this quilt.

Ocie Bish Shoup with her French friend

Basket
c. 1865
70 x 79 inches
Caroline Hazlett Thompson
(1845–1885)

BASKET QUILTS TURNED UP FREQUENTLY DURING THE DOCUMENTATION PHASE OF *Threads of Tradition: Northwest Pennsylvania Quilts.* This particular Basket quilt has a definite orientation, with one-half of the baskets facing the other half. It was made by Caroline Hazlett ("Haslet" in the 1850 census) Thompson, the daughter of Theodore and Mary Hazlett of Venango County. The quilt was made about 1865, approximately the time that Caroline wed Daniel Thompson, a farmer, of Shippenville. Raising seven children, they remained there all their lives. Caroline died December 19, 1885. The quilt has descended to Caroline's great-granddaughter, Regina Ion Sacolic.

Caroline Hazlett Thompson

Crawford County

*M*eadville, the first permanent post-Revolutionary settlement in northwest Pennsylvania, had its nearest neighbors at the forts of Waterford and Franklin, both with transient military and trader populations. Crawford County's earliest dwellings were log cabins and log houses, but the arrival in 1795 of a journeyman carpenter set families to building frame dwellings. By 1800 discovery of a good clay deposit made possible the production of a salmon-pink brick in sufficient quantities for home building; a quarry north of Allegheny College provided stone for foundations. In the first decade a dame school and an "English" school appeared. By 1805 an academy had opened, and in 1815 the cornerstone for Allegheny College was laid. A typical self-sufficient Atlantic seaboard community emerged by 1825, despite its distance from Buffalo and Pittsburgh, the nearest major urban centers.

During the early years poor roads and only marginally navigable waterways made the import of heavy goods difficult and expensive. Most furniture was locally made from the abundant hardwoods.

Storage items of wood or leather made turners, joiners, cabinet-makers, and tanners vital members of the community. Women made most of their textiles, cured food for the long winters, and harvested herbs and medicinals to season their diet and treat their families' illnesses.

The 1837 opening of the French Creek Feeder Canal to the mainline Beaver and Lake Erie Canal in the western part of the county, as well as the feeder's slackwater division east from Shaw's Landing to the Allegheny River, made possible the transport of raw materials and manufactured metal goods and thus the development of local foundries. By the early 1860s the opening of the Atlantic and Great Western Railroad, linking the port of New York to midwestern markets, put the area on an equal footing with Pennsylvania's major urban areas in its access to consumer goods.

Early housewives had spun their own thread and yarn from the wool and flax easily available in the county's agricultural economy. The earliest tax records list the fulling mills that processed the home-woven "linsey-woolsey" into a firm workable fabric and the "oil mills" that, in a waste-not-want-not lifestyle, made discarded flax seeds into linseed oil. The early introduction of merino sheep with their long, fine, soft fleece made the area a major woolen center well into the late-nineteenth century, and schools were established to train young people for textile mill work. Crawford County's climate required warm winter wear, and the locally made woolens were gratefully utilized.

Locally produced linen was commonly used for underclothing and for shirts and summer wear. Since linen fabrics in their last stages of wear were a "cash crop" bought by newspapers and others who made paper and paper-related products, the production of quilts may have competed with the need for hard money in cash-poor families. Every early issue of the *Crawford Weekly Messenger* (1805–1834) advertises cash for rags.

The self-sufficiency of the community, and indeed of the individual household, is well illustrated by the premium book of the First Annual Fair of the Crawford County Central Agricultural Society in 1856. It lists categories for such things as the best ten yards of (wool) flannel, the best pair of blankets, the best woolen carpet, and the best ten yards of domestic linen. Separate categories were listed for fabric products of local mills. Prizes were also offered for the best grass bonnets and the best straw hats! There were two categories for quilts: "best worked quilts" and "best patch-work quilts."

The home and local mill production of fabric continued well into the nineteenth century, but the instigation of direct rail links to major markets brought a wider variety of yard goods and manufactured cloth items to the county. Cottons and silks became more generally available. The boroughs and small villages remained the market and social centers for the farming areas in the later half of the nineteenth and early twentieth centuries, but access to railheads and commercial centers at Meadville and Titusville greatly improved, and the flow of manufactured fabrics in greater variety and of modern conveniences such as sewing machines increased after the Civil War.

As the twentieth century dawned and the county's population grew, better roads and more bridges made travel easier. Labor-saving devices such as charcoal-heated, crank-turned wringer washing machines made by Beierschmitt at Meadville, appeared, and carpet sweepers replaced brooms in the housewife's age-old fight against tracked-in dirt. Textile related industries sprang up, based not on the flax and wool base of the nineteenth century agricultural economy but on the manufacturing and entrepreneurial drive of hookless fasteners, flexible steel corset stays, and the new, rayon yarns.

Meanwhile, school, church, and social institutions such as the Grange, Odd Fellows, and service

INTERIOR VIEW OF

THE HOWE MACHINE CO's.,
OFFICE
GENERAL AGENCY FOR NORTH WESTERN PENN♀.

THE HOWE COMPANY SOLD OVER 250,000 MORE
MACHINES SINCE 1865, THAN ANY OF ITS COMPETITORS.
IT IS THE MOST RELIABLE AND THE MOST DURABLE OF
ALL SEWING MACHINES.

B.F. PORTER, GENERAL AGT.
RICHMOND'S BLOCK
MEADVILLE, PA.

From
Combination Atlas Map
of Crawford County
Pennsylvania,
1876

clubs created linkages for both men and women, with a resulting increase in social contact for formerly isolated families. At the turn of the century, newspapers multiplied as did the number of periodicals on both the county and national level. Soon the car, as well as radio and universal telephone access, further eliminated the isolation of rural families. With increased mobility, some of the impetus for remembrance and friendship quilts faded, as removal to Iowa, or Oregon, or even overseas no longer appeared as a major barrier to the continuation of friendships or family relationships.

Modern fabrics, better heating, home insulation, easy communication, and the continuing prosperity of the county, which was little impacted by the economic depression of the 1930s, tended to displace the incentives of economic hardship and physical discomfort that had driven quilt production in the area's early years.

— ANNE W. STEWART

From
*Combination Atlas Map
of Crawford County
Pennsylvania,
1876*

THE COMMUNITY OF TRYONVILLE (STEUBEN TOWNSHIP) HAS ROOTS THAT EXTEND TO THE
early days of Crawford County. Though both Artemisia Stedman and
David Tryon were natives of Litchfield, Connecticut, they married in 1828
in the community that adopted his family name. The first of Artemisia's
and David's eleven children was Mary Jane, born April 24, 1829. She
married Warner H. Waid in Centerville. He was the son of Warner and
Susan Patten Waid, whose ancestors were the first European settlers in
Randolph Township (Guys Mills). The first daughter, born to Warner and
Mary Jane in 1857, was Christiana Adah, who nicknamed herself
"Tannie." The couple's second daughter, Alice Maud, came along early in
1862. When Mary Jane died on April 6, 1865, the three- and eight-year-
old girls went to live with their aunts, Mary Jane's sisters, Arabella (Belle)
and Ella, at the Tryon family home. After the girls grew up they moved to
California, where they are both buried. The Tryons were "pioneer Methodists" as were the Waids. Tannie married Wellington Bowser, who graduated from Allegheny College and became a Methodist minister. In 1879
he and Tannie went to India as missionaries. Mary Jane made her Nine
Patch Basket quilt in the late 1840s. She may have begun the basket-quilt
fad that continued into the twentieth century, as basket patterns prevail in
northwestern Pennsylvania. Her extremely small baskets have not,
however, been replicated. The fragile brown backing of the quilt appears
to have been dyed with butternut or walnut shells. This quilt is from the
Collections of the Baldwin-Reynolds House Museum, Crawford County
Historical Society.

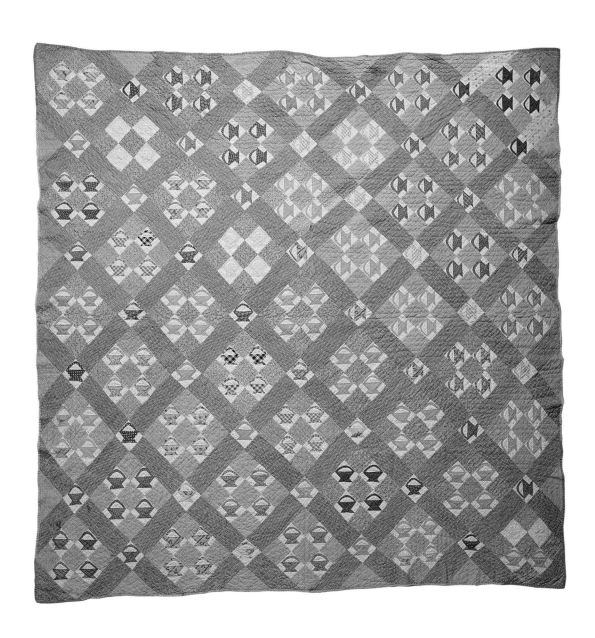

Nine Patch Basket
c. 1840s
78 x 76 inches
Mary Jane Tryon Waid (1829–1865)

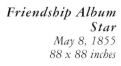

*Friendship Album
Star*
May 8, 1855
88 x 88 inches

THESE TWO FRIENDSHIP ALBUM STAR QUILTS ARE SOMETIMES CALLED "THE TWINS," ALBEIT
fraternal. They were made from the same basic pattern by some of the
same women in Meadville. Amazingly, they were donated to the Crawford
County Historical Society within a year of each other, from Kinnelon and
Newark, New Jersey.

The blue-calico-and-white quilt with sawtooth border is dated May 8,
1855, and contains forty-seven signatures. Friends and relatives who signed
the quilt include Grandma Baldwin, Mary A. Burnside, Mary Clemson
(for whom the multicolored quilt was made), Mr. and Mrs. Culbertson,
Mrs. Mary J. Finney, Mr. and Mrs. Andrew Grimes, Mrs. Hazelet, Maggie
D. Shaffer, and Mrs. Annie Smith (she also signed the other quilt). Family
tradition relates that the quilt was made for an "Aunt Nellie" dying of
tuberculosis at age twenty-seven, but Nellie K. Myers, likely the aunt of
tradition, lived from 1858 to 1886, her birthday postdating the quilt. It
may instead have been made as a wedding gift for Nellie's parents, Ellen
(or Ellenor) M. Liebhart and James S. Myers, married in 1855. Nellie
predeceased her mother, but her sisters, May B., Bernice M., Gertrude,
and Martha (Mattie) owned the quilt at one time and kept it in a trunk.

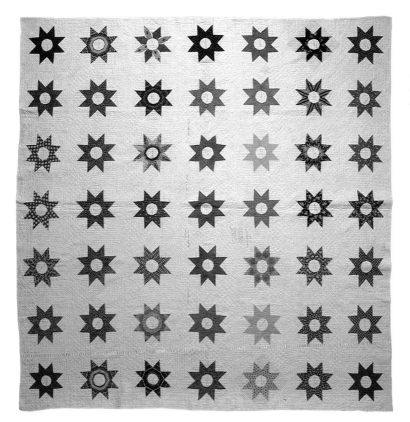

*Friendship Album
Star*
April 1858
83 x 87 inches
Friends of Mary M. Clemson
(1832–1907)

Martha was only four when her mother died at age fifty-four, and she too died young, at age twenty-eight, leaving twin daughters, Bernice Margaret and Eleanor, and a son, Orrin, whom Aunts May and Bernice raised. (Martha and Gertrude married and left the area, and Martha died at her sister's home in 1912 while she was visiting with the twins—-then two years old.)

The multicolored Friendship Album Star quilt is dated April 1858 and is thought to have been made by a church circle in Meadville, most likely for Mary M. Clemson. The eldest child of Rachel Burnside and Thomas Clemson, Mary was born on September 14, 1832. She was a teacher in the public schools from 1855 until the early 1860s. After her death in 1907, she was laid to rest with her parents in Greendale Cemetery. Her obituary in the *Crawford Journal* noted: "Many of our best citizens laid the foundation of their education under her guidance." It also extolled her "intelligence and Christian character." Mary had three sisters: Jane (Janie) Clemson Howe, Amanda Clemson Rea, and Anna Clemson Culbertson (see page 18). Prominent Meadville folks who signed the quilt include Henry C. Bates, Mrs. Eliza Gelvin, Sarah Kirkpatrick, Mrs. Anna Smith,

Martha (Mattie) Myers

Mrs. Adeline Snowden, several members of the Burnside family (Mary's mother's kin), Catherine Myers, and Mrs. Myers (see blue & white Friendship Album Star), and members of the Miniss family. In addition, the multicolored quilt carries this inscription: "To Mary, A token of friendship from your Meadville friends." The quilt was passed down through Amanda Clemson and Franklin Philander Rea's son, Robert M., to his second cousin Nancy Ray Fahnoe, who gave it to the Crawford County Historical Society in 1994.

Both quilts show this poem written in the center in indelible ink:

The earth can boast no purer tie
No richer, brighter gem
No jewel of lovelier die
Than friendships diadem

Thus may this ray of light divine
Never from our bosoms fade
But may it on our pathway shine
Till death our hearts invade

This kind of rhyme can be found in albums and/or autograph books of the era, thus the name given the quilts—Friendship Album. Both are in the Collections of the Baldwin-Reynolds House Museum, Crawford County Historical Society.

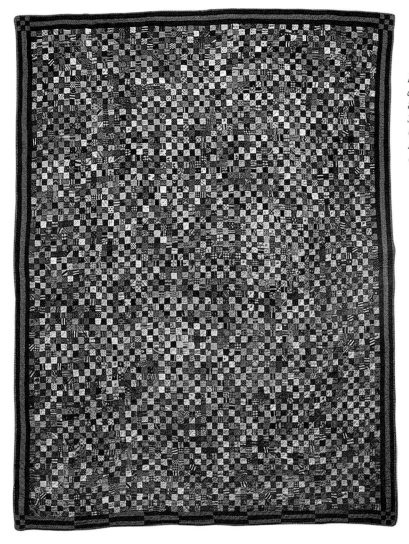

Postage Stamp
c. 1880–1890
86 x 64 inches
Sally Billings Phelps
(1806–1887)
Mary Hunt Phelps
(1835–1896)

THIS POSTAGE STAMP QUILT WAS MADE IN LINESVILLE, ON THE WESTERN EDGE OF THE COUNTY, very near Ohio. Chester Phelps, who donated the quilt to the Crawford County Historical Society, said there are five thousand tiny postage-stamp-sized pieces in the quilt. He was unsure whether his grandmother Mary Hunt Phelps (1835–1896) or great-grandmother Sally Billings Phelps (1806–1887) had made it, but thought it was quilted c. 1880–90. Perhaps Sally and Mary made it together. The Phelpses, who came to Crawford County in 1847, were farmers who ran a cheese factory. They were originally from Herkimer County, New York. The quilt is from the Collections of the Baldwin-Reynolds House Museum, Crawford County Historical Society.

Princess Feather
c. 1860
86 x 84 inches
Priscilla Yocum Weikel
(1839–1923)

PRISCILLA YOCUM MADE THIS STRIKING RED AND GREEN PRINCESS FEATHER QUILT IN HAYFIELD

Priscilla Yocum Weikel
with her granddaughter,
Hazel Woodring

Township. Born July 11, 1839, she was the daughter of Adam and Nancy Dunn Yocum, early settlers of the area. Priscilla married widower Daniel Weikel, a farmer, on July 3, 1860, in McGoffin Falls, Hayfield Township (Littles Corners), on French Creek. The quilt likely was made around this time. Priscilla and Daniel had a daughter, Gertrude, and were members of the Methodist Episcopal Church in Woodcock. When Priscilla died on February 17, 1923, she was survived by her daughter, Gertrude Woodring, and her granddaughter, Hazel Woodring, who later married Wallace Ernst. Exactly what inspired Priscilla to use the Princess Feather—an American derivation from "Prince's Feather," a red flower possibly named for the Prince of Wales—and particularly the tasseled-swag motif on the border, is not known. But with train transportation and institutions such as the opera houses in Conneautville, Meadville, and Titusville bringing in road shows, folks were certainly connected with the culture and material elegance available in major cities. The quilt is now in the collection of Aundra Swope Zack.

Oakleaf Variation
c. 1897
90 x 88 inches
Lulu Jeanette Blair Knight
(1878–1973)

LULU JEANETTE BLAIR MADE THIS EXCEPTIONAL OAKLEAF VARIATION QUILT ABOUT 1897, WHEN she was in her late teens. The intertwined vine on the wide border is stuffed, as are the berries and leaves. The indigo fabric is calico, and the quilting is extraordinary. A former owner of the quilt described Lulu Jeanette Blair as "imaginative and artistic and generally skilled in household arts." The Blair family has roots in Crawford County extending to 1802, when Hugh and Jane Blair emigrated from County Antrim, Ireland. The daughter of Mr. and Mrs. Andrew Blair, Lulu married Lt. Col. William Knight at her parents' home on Main Street in Meadville, with the pastor of First Presbyterian Church officiating. The April 30, 1906, wedding was eloquently described in the *The Meadville Daily Messenger*. After the wedding dinner, the young couple "departed on the evening train for New York and other eastern cities." In 1907 Lulu and William became the parents of a daughter, Helen Louise, who later worked as a librarian. Both Lulu's husband, a World War I veteran, and her father, a veteran of the Civil War, were telegraphers on the Erie Railroad. Lulu belonged to the First Presbyterian Church and was a charter member of the Meadville Women's Club. Lulu died at age ninety-five in 1973. The quilt is now in the collection of Aundra Swope Zack.

Lulu Jeanette
Blair Knight

Edna Bently Haight
with her children:
Alice (holding violin)
Margaret (seated)
Mary (floor)
Berneice (Edna's lap)
and Donald (daybed)
1900

Westward migration was commonplace in the mid-nineteenth century, but it was
nonetheless a traumatic experience. This Friendship quilt was finished
November 20, 1898, according to the square constructed by Mary
Wilder. The quilt was made for Edna Bentley Haight by her relatives and
friends in the Guys Mills Congregational Church after she "removed" to
Iowa in the 1890s, so that Edna would always remember the community
"back home." Edna went west with her dentist husband, Dr. Penrose D.
Haight, and their six children. Both Edna and Penrose penned their names
on the quilt, perhaps before they left. Edna never did come home again as
she died prematurely in 1908. After she died, the doctor and eldest son
Frank went off to Canada; Edna's sister, Alice Marilla Bentley, went to
Iowa to fetch the younger children—Margaret, Alice (Haight), Donald,
Mary, Berneice—and the quilt. She brought them back to Guys Mills
where relatives cared for them. The children's Aunt Alice was then living
in Meadville, where, after teaching school for twenty years, she became a
businesswoman. Alice would have been considered a "New Woman" as
she was single, outspoken, and independent. She was an advocate of
women's rights and became one of Pennsylvania's first female legislators
(three were elected in 1922). The quilt is executed in the red embroidery
thread typical of the day, but the use of black for the profile of Mrs.
Benjamin Harrison, then First Lady, is a bit curious. Perhaps the embroi-
derer chose the black thread to simulate a silhouette. The "baby" of the
family, Berneice Haight Patterson, lived to be ninety-nine and bequeathed
her mother's Friendship quilt to her daughter, Mary Beth Patterson
Hagamen, M.D.

Friendship
November 20, 1898
88 x 74 inches
Members of the Guys Mills Congregational Church

Phoebe Swift Humes (left) and Leatha Humes

THE GUYS MILLS AREA (RANDOLPH TOWNSHIP) HAS ENJOYED STRONG ROOTS IN CHRISTIANITY.

Guys Mills Methodist Episcopal Church

When Leatha Humes was a young girl in 1937–38, her mother, Phoebe Swift Humes, taught her Sunday School class at the Guys Mills Methodist Episcopal Church. Phoebe decided that making a Friendship quilt would be a good class project and would teach the girls to create something special from what was on hand. Phoebe asked each girl to bring fabric left from making her favorite dress for the dress of the "girl" on the quilt. She sketched the pattern (on stationery from the Hotel McAlpin in Philadelphia) and planned to make thirteen personalized little-girl blocks with twelve white filler blocks. Leatha had other plans. She wanted every block to be appliquéd so she could include a block for her grandmother, several aunts, the pastor's wife, and neighbors, and *two* blocks for herself. Her mother, who had been widowed when Leatha was a toddler, acquiesced. Phoebe did put her foot down when Leatha wanted to quilt the entire quilt, saying it would take too long and she would get too tired. Thus Leatha quilted the top three rows and Phoebe, her friends, and relatives did the rest. Perhaps when Leatha put down her needle and thimble, she dreamed about the faraway places she would someday see. She graduated from college, earned two master's degrees, then became a missionary in Indonesia. In 1980 Leatha received a doctorate from Gordon-Conwell Divinity School. She returned to Guys Mills to care for Phoebe in her advancing years. After Phoebe's death at age ninety-three in 1991, Leatha returned to Indonesia where she teaches and writes curriculum for children. Because she is so far away and has no descendants, Leatha has gave her quilt to her friend Cheryl Seber Weiderspahn.

Friendship
1937–38
78 x 68 inches
Phoebe Swift Humes (1897–1991), Leatha Humes
(1925), and Guys Mills Methodist Episcopal Church
Sunday School Class

Erie County

$\mathcal{D}$uring the years when the Erie Indians roamed the area along Lake Erie between what are now Toledo, Ohio, and Buffalo, New York, they followed the rulings of Queen Gegosasa. As "mother of nations" she used diplomacy to settle hostilities between the Wyandotte and the Iroquois.

Queen Gegosasa may have made a practice of meditation, especially if she observed the native custom of retreating to a lodge of separation during menstruation (page 30). While at the lodge, a woman performed only light labor. Superstition decreed that everything touching her hands during this time was unclean. Woe to the hunter or warrior whose step crossed hers. Queen Gegosasa's reign ended in 1654, when the Iroquois rejected one of her peace proposals, then (successfully) waged war

Menstrual Lodge

From *Information Respecting the History Condition and Prospects of the Indian Tribes of the United States*, Vol. V, by Henry R. Schoolcraft, 1855

against the Eries. The French came to terms with the Iroquois long enough to build forts at Erie, Waterford, and Venango, but the English drove them away. The Iroquois retaliated, and the area remained theirs until Gen. Anthony Wayne subdued them in 1794.

On July 5, 1795, Hannah Harwood Reed and Seth Reed and two sons arrived at Erie. Hannah, prepared with bedding and a cask of whiskey, is credited with suggesting that they expand their crude log cabin into a hotel. Other families came to settle in Union Township, North East, Edinboro, and Fairview, and land disputes were frequent. Every house had a spinning wheel, and many had looms, but local women did much more: housewife Isabella Nicholson, for instance, personally burned the bricks for her fourth residence/inn, and she could use a squirrel rifle with accuracy.

During the War of 1812, the town of four hundred residents grew as three hundred marine workers came to build Commodore Oliver Hazard Perry's fleet. Erie women obliged when he requested a flag with the motto, "Don't Give Up the Ship." After the battle, women in Erie and Waterford nursed the wounded.

Merchant Rufus Reed, son of Hannah and Seth, and sailing master Daniel Dobbins continued to lead Erie's development as a port city. Mills, distilleries, banks, and other supporting services developed. Inns, in particular, relied on women to maintain cleanliness and cook good food.

In 1808, when Fairview established a Presbyterian church, the proposition of the arrival of Elizabeth Canon Eaton, the new minister's wife, caused one member to say, "We don't want any plaything for a wife in these woods." They found upon meeting her that she was sensible and affable—far from a plaything. As Erie developed churches, Mrs. Judah Colt and her friends started the first Sunday schools in 1822. When Lafayette toured the area in 1823, the Waterford women proudly supplied a banquet. In later years runaway slaves found resting places offered by such women as Mrs. Josiah Kellogg.

Whiskey! Trouble! Wattsburg established the first Prohibition Society in 1829. Wesleyville women destroyed a tavern, and in 1853, ninety-nine women in Erie and Wattsburg petitioned for a prohibitory liquor law.

The building of the Erie Extension Canal, better roads, and the arrival of the railroad (with much controversy) helped Erie reach the status of a city in 1851. The adjacent areas of North East, Fairview, Girard, and Edinboro emphasized fruit farming and agriculture. During the Civil War women formed Ladies Aid Societies to help families and soldiers. When peace came, groups such as Albion's Women's Relief Corps assisted families of veterans.

The discovery of oil in 1859 in Pithole made a boomtown of nearby Corry. Muddy streets meant extra labor for women. The Climax Locomotive Company became a major employer in Corry. And women found employment opportunities when the NuBone Corset company set up business in 1910.

By 1830 Erie had established academies for both men and women, and it opened a public high school in 1866. One of its first graduates, Adella B. Woods, went on to become a physician. St. Benedict Academy for girls began in 1870, and Villa Academy in 1892. The Sisters of St. Joseph first operated an orphanage, then built St. Vincent's Hospital in 1875. Hamot Hospital joined the scene in 1881, supported especially by the women of St. Paul's Episcopal Church. Children and older women became the focus when Sarah Reed joined with twenty-nine other women to establish The Home for the Friendless in 1871. Meanwhile in Edinboro, the establishment of a teacher training Institute in 1856 became central to the town's development and to the county's supply of school-teachers. A model for physical education programs for women was created by Nettie Mae Ruttle in 1929. She advocated health measures such as pasteurization of milk and a clean water system.

Laura Sanford wrote the first history of Erie County in 1861, while Girard supported culture with its Chautauqua Study Group as early as 1880. Artist Lovisa Card-Catlin established an art school and organized the Erie Art Club in 1898. The growth of the Erie Playhouse, Erie Philharmonic, ballet, the Daughters of the American Revolution, libraries, and professional groups such as Zonta also engaged women.

Two major companies, Hammermill Paper Company (1897) and General Electric Company (1909) speeded Erie's industrial growth. Women worked assembly lines during World War I, but not until World War II did banks employ women tellers. Then, too, women joined the military—as WACS, WAVES, and WAAFS. Both wars also brought ethnic changes, with immigrants taking factory and farm jobs. In North East, Maidee Olson pioneered in the language instruction of many Italian immigrants. Erie's International Institute provided services such as aid to immigrants seeking citizenship. Women voted in 1927, helping Maud Miller win the post of city treasurer. Helen Schluraff began a twelve-year term as a county commissioner in 1932.

Educational institutions multiplied, with Villa Maria and Mercyhurst Colleges for Women starting in the mid-1920s, followed by Gannon College in 1939. Gertrude Barber, M.D., began her work with students having special needs, and Erie Business College continued the programs initiated by Clark Business School in 1894. Erie's beautiful Presque Isle became a state park in 1925, with Annie Scott Strong on the original board. Here the Red Cross worked for water-safety programs, and volunteer nurses "manned" a first-aid hut. By 1940 Erie County had a diverse base ready to meet the challenges yet to come.

— M A R G A R E T   L .   T E N P A S

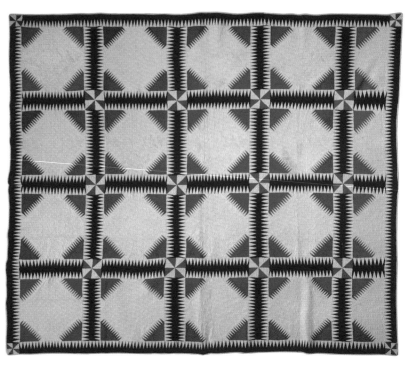

*Rocky Mountain
Road*
Pieced 1852, quilted 1857
102½ x 87 inches
Margaret Steeley Kelley
(1784–1865)

DURING THE HEIGHT OF WESTWARD MIGRATION IN THE 1850S, ROCKY MOUNTAIN ROAD

Detail

naturally became a popular pattern. Margaret Steeley Kelley moved westward, though not as far as many women. Perhaps the rocky roads of the Alleghenies were what she remembered after settling in Erie County in the early years of the nineteenth century. Margaret and her husband, John Kelley, were both born in Lewistown, Pennsylvania. Family legend discloses the story of the young couple braving the wilds of western Pennsylvania on horseback, with Margaret holding their baby girl, Cartus E. Kelley (later Webb). Though eleven children were born to the couple, only seven were reported living in 1884, after John and Margaret had died. In the 1860 census the couple was listed as living in Girard with two sons, William S. and Lazarus S., and one daughter, Mary J., who attended school. John, a veteran of the War of 1812, made his living as a farmer. In Girard Margaret pieced the top of her Rocky Mountain Road quilt, but she credited Janet Amanda Coates, perhaps a professional quilter, for the tiny stitches that hold top, batting, and back together. The filler blocks are each intricately quilted with a tree and bird motif . Margaret intended this quilt to be a historical document, as it is inscribed with the words, "Pieced 1852 Quilted 1857." Margaret was born August 8, 1794, and died May 19, 1865. Margaret and John's granddaughter Mary Adelaide Kelley donated the quilt to the Erie Historical Museum.

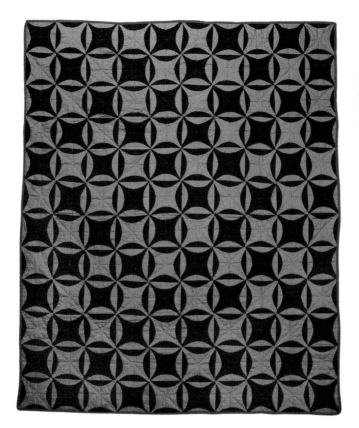

Orange Peel
c. 1918
83 x 67 inches
Fred Irving Kimball
(1860–1928)

FRED IRVING KIMBALL'S MOTHER, LOUISA BICKFORD KIMBALL, MADE THE BEST OF A TRAGIC situation. She was left a young widow with two small sons after her husband was killed by an ox when working in the fields. Louisa was an excellent seamstress who put her talents to work, sewing professionally after her husband's death. At the time Fred was approximately two years old. When Fred and his brother became old enough to use the needle, they helped their mother with the sewing. Fred grew up and attended Fredonia Normal School, where he trained to be a schoolteacher. A woman with whom he boarded taught the nimble-fingered lad to quilt. This hobby extended past his marriage, when he made this Orange Peel quilt for his daughter, Vivian, sometime before her thirteenth birthday, in about 1918. Fred was born in French Creek, New York, in 1860 and married Vivian's mother, Sara Anna Evans, in 1887. They lived in the country east of North East, and moved into town later in life. After some years of teaching school, Fred went into business. Fred and Sara Anna had three other daughters: Edna Marie, Velma, and Luella, and family tradition indicates Fred made each of them a quilt. Fred died in 1928, but his legacy continues through Kimball men, as the quilt is now owned by his grandson Meryl Kimball Bemiss.

Fred Irving Kimball

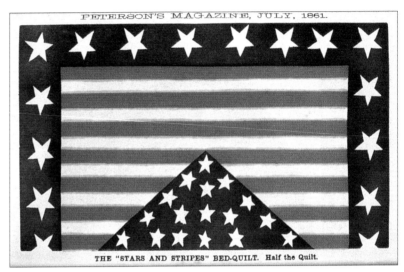

PETERSON'S MAGAZINE, JULY, 1861.

THE "STARS AND STRIPES" BED-QUILT. Half the Quilt.

Courtesy of the Smithsonian Institution ©1996

FROM JULY 4, 1861, UNTIL JULY 4, 1863, THIRTY-FOUR STATES COMPRISED THE UNION, AND quiltmaker Emaline P. Sackett Hayt celebrated that fact with this bold Stars and Stripes quilt. The thirty-four appliquéd stars in the center represent the number of states when she made her quilt in 1862, but the thirty-six stars on the border are somewhat puzzling. When Emaline saw the pattern in the July 1861 issue of *Peterson's Magazine*, a periodical for women, she likely went posthaste to buy her fabric. In addition to providing the date, she signed her name and the name of the town McKean (where she lived). Family tradition tells us that the quilt was once exhibited at an Erie museum. Emaline was originally from Munson Township, Ohio, though Sackett's Harbor (Erie) no doubt was connected with her family in some way. This lake port played a primary role in the War of 1812. Emaline moved to McKean after her marriage on November 8, 1840, to Charles Hayt, a pioneer lake captain and farmer. In 1866 Charles bought a farm with a sturdy brick home in Springfield Township to use as a summer residence. His Union roots, extending twelve years earlier than Emaline's, were in Massachusetts. The couple became the parents of four daughters: Rosilla E., Rosina E., Mary R., and Eva J. Emaline celebrated her fortieth birthday the year she made her quilt. She died in Erie in 1887 when she was sixty-five. Patricia A. Pochatko now owns this significant Civil-War-era quilt.

Stars and Stripes
1862
85 x 83 inches
Emaline P. Sackett Hayt
(1822–1887)

Spider Web
c. 1916
83 x 80 inches
Maude Briggs Zahner
(1874–1975)

MAUDE BRIGGS ZAHNER WAS AN AVID QUILTER WHOSE LONGEVITY PROVIDED HER THE TIME TO

Maude Briggs Zahner,
March 22, 1964

be a prolific quiltmaker as well. Maude was born in Michigan on March 22, 1874, and survived to age 101; she died on April 9, 1975. Maude's parents, both of whom were born in the United States, were of English heritage. Maude's husband, Gustave Frederick Zahner, was born in Switzerland. As a boy he emigrated to Michigan with his parents and siblings, where he met Maude. They married in Chicago on October 12, 1893, subsequently becoming the parents of two sons, and one daughter. Though she resided in Michigan at the time of her birth and death, Maude spent most of her adult life in Erie. She may have learned to quilt in Youngstown, Ohio, where she lived after her marriage. There her sister-in-law Lottie Brightman Briggs and Lottie's mother belonged to a quilting group at a Baptist church. After moving to Erie in 1915, Maude made her Spider Web quilt, perhaps aided by her widowed mother, Ester Mueller Briggs, who lived with her then. Maude's grandson Richard Zahner now owns this quilt, one of twenty known to exist by her hand.

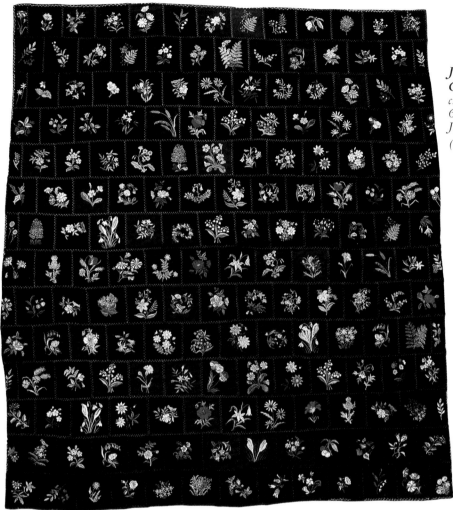

*Josephine's
Garden*
c. 1900–1925
66 x 60 inches
Josephine W. Tetzlaff
(–1946)

JOSEPHINE'S GARDEN IS AN ORIGINAL PATTERN THAT JOSEPHINE W. TETZLAFF CONCEIVED FROM observing the flowers in her garden. Each five-inch black wool square has a different plant embroidered within the small space. Each resembles a botanical print, and more than 168 plants are represented. Josephine's Garden was made in the first quarter of the twentieth century. Josephine and her husband, John, were the parents of Catherine, who donated this specimen to the Erie Historical Museum when Josephine died in 1946. Catherine worked at the Erie Public Library and no doubt understood the importance of preservation.

*Theresa Hannah Abt Zuerl
with her family:
standing, left to right,
Helena, Heinrich, Emilie
and seated, left to right,
Friedrich Wilhelm,
Margaret Elisabeth,
and Theresa*

ALTHOUGH SUNBONNET SUE APPLIQUÉ PATTERNS FIRST APPEARED IN 1910, THEY BECAME popular only in the early 1920s. When Theresa Hannah Abt Zuerl made her Sunbonnet Sue quilt, she intertwined two themes and created an original design with the use of bonnets as a border. The themes are Sunbonnet Sue and the tasks assigned to each day of the week. Sue is obviously dressed for Sunday-go-to-meeting, all decked out in a red coat and red bonnet (perhaps not a sunbonnet in winter) with a muff. All of this is topped off with "fake" ermine trim. The other Sues wash, iron, market, sweep, and dust, but more play appears than in the rhyme most of us remember. Theresa made the quilt for her granddaughter Anne Elizabeth Hubbel Evansoff; perhaps she wanted the little girl to know that all work and no play makes a dull child. Theresa likely saw little play during the middle years of her life when she reared the five children (four of whom were living at the time the photo above was taken) she and her husband, Frederick Wilhelm Zuerl, created together. Theresa was born in 1844 in Switzerland, and Frederick in 1831 in Bavaria. They were married in Erie in 1875; they were Lutherans. Theresa made her heirloom quilt at about age eighty. When she died in 1935 she was a nonagenarian. Her quilt is now in the collection of Peg Weymer.

Sunbonnet Sue
86 x 73 inches
c. 1920–1925
Theresa Hannah Abt Zuerl (1844–1935)

Mercer County

In 1785 a company of men from Washington County trekked into the Third District of the Northwest Territory of Pennsylvania, which in 1800 became known as the county of Mercer, named for the Revolutionary hero Gen. Hugh Mercer. By official appointment, these men were commissioned to survey and map out several thousand acres of Donation Land in the territory, set aside to repay servicemen who saw action in the War of Independence. This virgin-forest–clad wilderness was then inhabited by Native-American tribes and such wild animals as bears, deer, wolves, wildcats, and buffalo. There was no trace of European civilization other than at the Moravian Mission outpost of Fort Venango (Franklin), located at the confluence of French Creek and the Allegheny River in Venango County.

One of the men in that group, Benjamin Stokley, returned to the area with his wife, Esther Alexander, in June 1796. They made their way to Cool Spring Township with their first three children. According to the 1888 *History of Mercer County*, Benjamin was not the first white man to live in the wilderness, but he was the only trader to settle there permanently at that time. Robert Richford Roberts, his sister Elizabeth Lindsay, and his brother Thomas also wended their way from

Westmoreland County over the Alleghenies in 1796 to settle in Salem Township (Leech's Corners), where they built a log house. Robert returned to Ligonier three years later to marry Mary Elizabeth Oldham and bring her back to Mercer County the same year. Roberts was ordained as a Methodist Episcopal minister in 1801 and was elected bishop in 1816. He and Mary Elizabeth, pioneering Methodists, opened their home as a school and center for Sunday worship.

Roberts and Stokley apparently had little in common. Some of Stokley's behavior was even considered "irreverent and eccentric." He had converted to Methodism early in his life (perhaps at Robert's hand) but soon became skeptical. He nevertheless showed up with a "yoke of oxen" to help build a church in Cool Spring (perhaps Robert's). Stokley reportedly said to those in attendance, "Here comes the devil to help build your church." After forty years as a non-believer, he again accepted the Christian doctrine.

The Axtells, another early Mercer County family (see page 47), settled in Sandy Creek Township before the turn of the nineteenth century. Daniel was closely identified with the Fairview Presbyterian Church, becoming a charter member in 1799. Seven children resulted from the union of Daniel and Ruth, and their son Daniel Jr. and his wife, Euphemia, further filled the pews of the Fairview church with their twelve young Axtells. Their first child, Ruth, born August 28, 1808, may have been the first white child born in the county. Axtell pioneers lived in Sheakleyville and Clarks Mills as well; many of them were Presbyterians. Annie M. Axtell was a charter member of the Georgetown Presbyterian Church.

Susan Dock Bigler emigrated to Delaware Township in 1817. She was widowed at an early age and reared ten children alone. Somehow Susan found the inspiration and time to piece and quilt a Log Cabin quilt, reminiscent perhaps of the first home she shared with her husband, Jacob. Two of Susan's sons became newspapermen and went on to serve their respective states in public office. John Bigler went west in 1849, to become the third governor of California. William Bigler remained in Pennsylvania, where he was inaugurated as the state's twelfth governor on January 20, 1852, the same day as brother John.

In the early days few girls attended the log schools, as it was believed they needed only to learn to spin, weave, sew, and take care of home and family. A change in their role was first realized during the War Between the States, when many were left behind to tend both home and farm, work in factories, and teach. When time permitted, women met to lend a hand to the outside world through missionary society work. As they stitched, knitted, and quilted, they vowed to work for better health care, the abolition of liquor traffic, and equal rights.

Word of opportunity spread abroad into Europe, and persons came hoping for a better way of life. These later settlers, who came primarily from England, Ireland, Scotland, Germany, and Holland, found work in factories, leaving the families of the first settlers with farming, the leading industry in Mercer County until 1940. Some local history is told through old letters and diaries, penned by flickering candlelight as well as legal papers and printed news reports. Quilts and coverlets, made for events of note, recorded the heartbeats of those who lived the experiences. Our grandmothers pieced and stitched their joys and trials, the warp and woof of living, into each heirloom.

In general, Mercer County mothers taught their daughters to sew, knit, spin, weave, and make butter, cheese, soap, and candles. The girls also milked cows, tended chickens, plucked goose-feathers for making featherbeds, helped make gardens, care for the family, and learned to do fieldwork. Only a few women became active in professions other than teaching. Hundreds of women have been honored for service in the log and octagon schools, the three hundred plank, frame, and brick rural one-roomers of Mercer County.

During the 1930s and other troubled economic depressions, women carried the burden of feeding, clothing, and caring for their own and other families. One stitch and then another has, however, produced many a masterpiece of history in Mercer County through the years since the Stokleys, Roberts, Zahnisers, Morelands, Alexanders, Carmichaels, Bentleys, Perrines, and hundreds of other families called this county home.

We often hear that "women's work is never done." But the women found satisfaction around the quilting frames, in providing quilts for both history and comfort, especially for children and grandchildren.

— JOANNIE APPLESEED
(MAE LITTLE BERINGER)

Harriet Ann Jewell Gordon with her parents and seven brothers

HARRIET ANN JEWELL MAY HAVE COMPLETED ONLY A GRADE-SCHOOL EDUCATION, BUT HER SENSE of, interest in, and knowledge of what was going on in the world was fantastic. She probably did not name this Embroidered Current Events quilt. The portraits she included are figures from the nineteenth century, and that she captured the images of so many women makes one wonder whether she was a woman's rights advocate. Considering that she grew up with seven brothers, she may have been! The quilt was made c. 1898 in Milledgeville. Harriet's mother taught her to quilt, and she may have been in her mother's company a long time as she did not marry James Gordon until age thirty-seven. They had no children. Some of the people and events Harriet etched with red embroidery thread are: "President Grover and Mrs. Cleveland, Frances Willard, William McKinley, Rev. J. D. and Mrs. J. D. Talmage, W. J. Bryan and Mary B. Bryan, and Belva Lockwood," the first woman nominated for the presidency of the United States. Harriet wrote and captured the images of "G. W. Carter killed by Walter Wheaton and Ned McKay," "Uncle Sam viewing Uncle Sam," and "Remember the *Maine*." As you can see, Harriet set the artistic portraits so whoever was making the bed could absorb the news on either side. Ina M. McClimans now owns the quilt.

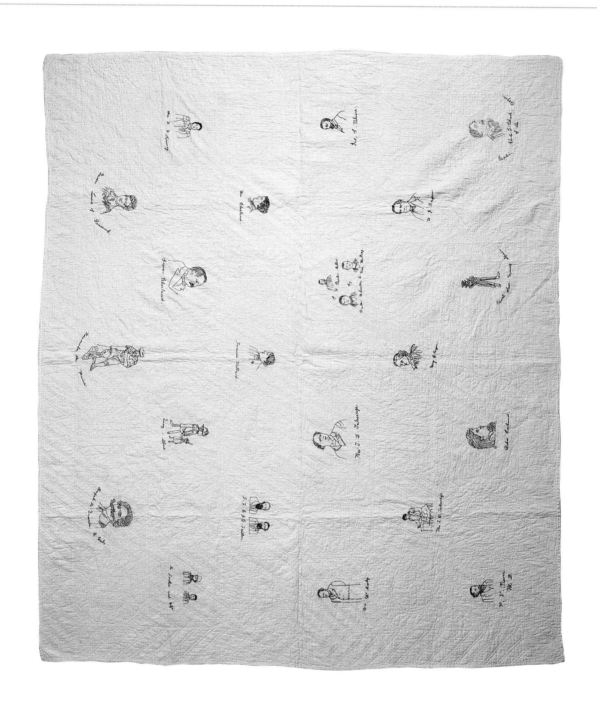

Embroidered Current Events
c. 1898
85 x 75 inches
Harriet Ann Jewell Gordon (1857–1941)

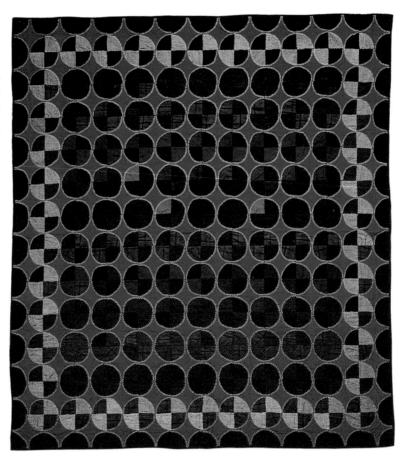

Steeple Chase
c. 1900
76 x 70 inches
Malinda Zook Ligo
(1863–1933)

NEW WILMINGTON HAS ENJOYED A LONG TRADITION OF AMISH SETTLERS, OF WHICH THE ZOOK

Malinda Zook Ligo (left)
with sisters Emma
(center) and Sarah
(right)

family was a part. Malinda Zook was born and reared in rural New Wilmington, but when she married C. Shephard Ligo, a Mennonite, she became "English." Actually Malinda worked for "Shep" before their marriage, when he was a widower with twins. She went to his home to care for the babies, but they both died, and Malinda stayed on and married Shep. After their marriage they had four children together—three girls and one boy. Shep was a farmer, and Malinda a home-maker. She made her Steeple Chase quilt, c. 1900; with a little imagination, one can conjure Malinda chasing steeples after leaving the Society of Plain People among whom she was reared. Malinda was born on September 14, 1863, and died April 4, 1933. The quilt was passed down to Malinda and Shep's grandson, the late Richard Moose, and his wife, Catheryn R. Moose.

Log Cabin/
Barn-raising
c. 1895
82 x 78 inches
Edith Elva (Elvie)
Snyder Clark
(1885–1974)

EDITH ELVA (ELVIE) SNYDER WAS BORN IN 1885 IN NEW VERNON TOWNSHIP AND LIVED there until she married Frank Lee Clark. Her mother, Euphemia Axtell Snyder, most likely did the greatest amount of work on the Log Cabin/Barn-raising quilt they made together, c. 1895, as Elvie would have been only about ten years old. The Axtell family tree has roots in the area extending to 1787 when Daniel Axtell Sr. emigrated to Sandy Creek. Elvie's mother and father, Archer Snyder, attended Carpenters Corners Church of Christ, where Elvie most likely married Frank Lee Clark. After their marriage in 1910, the young couple moved to Clarks Mills. They became the parents of Archer, Euphemia, Clara, and Marshall. Euphemia was an old family name noted in the mid-nineteenth century when Euphemia Lynn wed Daniel Axtell. Elvie is remembered in the twentieth century to have made at least two quilts, but her children recall her more clearly for the rugs she crocheted. Marshall and D. Jane Clark now own the quilt.

Edith Elva (Elvie) Snyder Clark

THESE WATER LILY AND CATTAIL QUILTS EMERGED FROM A PATTERN PUBLISHED IN THE 1930s by Mountain Mist. A milliner and seamstress whose parents were both born in Germany, Hilda Kruger McClellan brought a professional hand to the art of quilting. After her Irish husband, Walter Joseph McClellan, died, Hilda went to live with her son and daughter-in-law. When she made these quilts, she no doubt intended to give her son and daughter-in-law the bed-sized quilt and their infant daughter the crib quilt. But something happened, and the parents, Joseph and Leona, never received the larger one. Baby Janet did receive hers, and she used it well. Hilda was determined that another son, Walter, would get the quilt and thus sewed a message to that effect on a piece of muslin attached to the back. Janet, now grown, doesn't understand why her parents, with whom Hilda made her home, were not given the quilt. She believes there may have been some sort of disagreement. (We all understand how families can be.) Walter never had children, however, and after he died, his wife gave it to Janet M. Runkle, who happily now owns both quilts.

Hilda Kruger McClellan

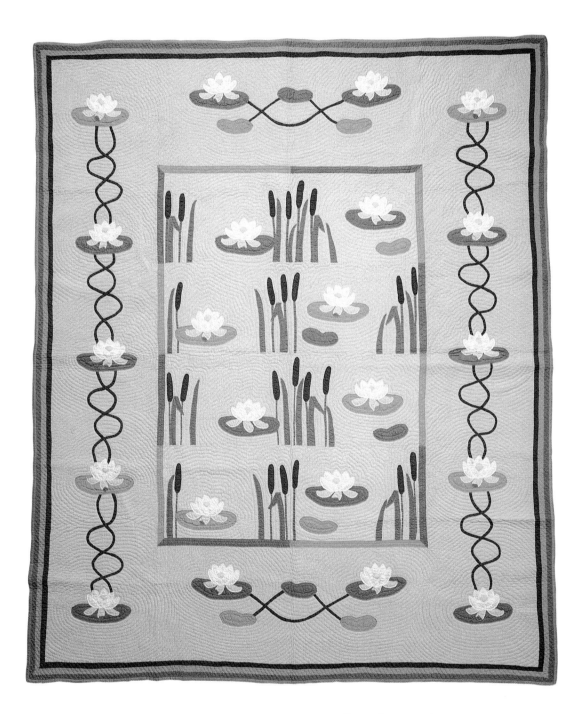

Water Lily and Cattail
c. 1935
94 x 78 inches and 58 x 36 inches
Hilda Kruger McClellan (1891–1987)

Crazy Quilt
1898
82 x 81 inches
Sophia Haner
(1856–1932)

SOPHIA HANER, CAUGHT UP IN THE FASHION FOR CRAZY QUILTS AT THE END OF THE NINETEENTH
century, produced at least three that have outlived her. This Crazy Quilt
shows many initials worked in with the intricate and decorative stitching
as well as the date, 1898, that it was made. Sophia got her ideas for the
many embroidery patterns she used from flower and seed catalogs and the
pictures seen in magazines. Feather stitching holds the twenty-five blocks
together, and an off-white ruffle surrounds the blocks keeping all the
crazy designs intact. Although Sophia was born in Otter Creek Township
in 1856, she was of German heritage. The man she later married, Michael
Haner, was born in the "old country" of Germany in 1851. He helped by
making quilting frames for Sophia. They were both Lutherans, and they
had two sons. Sophia taught her daughter-in-law, Grace Rath Haner, the
art of quilting, and she quilted with her neighbors at quilting bees. She
probably obtained the many signatures contained in this quilt at such
bees. Her friends may have helped her with this quilt, but she would have
made sure their stitches were "up to snuff." Whenever Sophia went
visiting or spent her time in what she considered a frivolous manner, she
made the time up in the evening by stitching her quilts by the light of the
kerosene or gas lamp. Saving her crazy quilts for overnight guests, Sophia
also made plain quilts for the family. Ethel Robinson now owns this quilt.

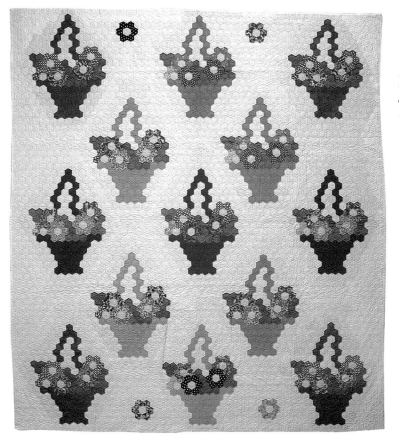

Flower Garden Basket
80 x 74 inches
c. 1920
Lottie Estella Polley Young
(1872–1959)

GRANDMOTHER'S FLOWER GARDEN QUILTS WERE POPULAR IN THE EARLY 1920S, BUT LOTTIE
Estella Polley Young chose to vary her flower garden by making it into baskets. She was born January 3, 1872, in Pymatuning Township, to Abner Polley and Lydia Rickert Polley, who were of German and Dutch ancestry. Their union brought forth eight children, six of whom lived to adulthood. Lottie was the fourth. Her three sisters likely quilted as well, and they may have contributed some stitches to Lottie's Flower Garden Basket quilt, c. 1920. Lottie had an excellent eye for color and matched the flower prints in symmetry within each basket. She married Robert Lincoln Young on September 11, 1894, and their family expanded to include five offspring. When Lottie died on December 5, 1959, she left four children, sisters Ollie and Jessie, eight grandchildren, eight great-grandchildren, and three great-great-grandchildren. Lottie's daughter Erma Mannozzi gave her flower-garden-variation quilt to her grandniece Evelyn Grabigel.

Lottie Estella Polley Young (far left)
with her sisters (left to right) Lizzie
Polley Reinhart, Jessie Polley Nicklin,
and Addie Polley Miles, 1958

Venango County

$\mathcal{V}$enango County has had several "pioneer" periods—times during which the women shared in trials and hardships as well as lent their spirits to the development of the region. They came as wives and as daughters when the first settlers arrived in the fading days of the eighteenth century and in the dawn of a new era after 1800. On horseback, by covered wagon, and on boats wending up the Allegheny River, they arrived to help tame this new land. Remnants of Fort Franklin remained in the settlement that was to become the county seat. Large tracts of rural land were provided for Revolutionary War veterans or offered at a nominal fee to those who would homestead and clear the woodland.

Women became adept at handling the hoe and the ax, at spinning wool, pulling flax, and weaving it into a sturdy cloth. They could skin a rabbit, salt bear and deer meat for winter, and dry corn and other vegetables; they gave birth and tended their babies, at the same time teaching the older children how to sew, cook, and plant seeds. They survived when the environment was hostile.

Sarah McDowell was a pioneer woman of the strongest ilk. Her husband, Col. Alexander McDowell, surveyor and agent for the Holland Land Company, had come in 1794, building a log

Allegheny River
From
*Information Respecting
the History Condition and
Prospects of the Indian Tribes
of the United States*, Part IV,
by Henry R. Schoolcraft,
1855

cabin near French Creek at Franklin. Sarah arrived three years later. Accustomed to the comforts of a fine Philadelphia home, she quickly adapted to new surroundings. She became friends with Chief Cornplanter and other Native Americans of the region, who would trade her a nice-sized fish for a coin. She raised chickens and gardened. When she saw a chicken eating some prized melon seeds, she sprang into action. With scissors she carefully cut open the chicken's craw, squeezed out the precious contents, then sewed up the wound with needle and thread. The hen survived to produce more eggs, and the seeds were planted to produce more melons. (See page 79.)

The first pioneer women were instrumental in establishing the moral fiber of their communities and in helping start churches and schools. Another wave of pioneer women came to Venango County during the boom that followed the success of the world's first oil well in 1859. Col. Edwin L. Drake's driller was "Uncle Billy" Smith, whose daughter, Margaret, cooked for her father and brother in the rustic lease house built at the well site. Many families followed husbands and fathers to these makeshift homes, hoping for new prosperity.

When Frank Tarbell moved his family to the boomtown of Rouseville in the 1860s, his children attended a school set up in the home of a Mrs. Rice. Tarbell's wife, Esther, was among those who worked to make the community "fit for self-respecting families." Her daughter, Ida Tarbell (born in Hatch Hollow, Erie County), later recalled: "There was a good deal that was militant in this effort to make a decent community. My mother had it in her to be a first-class crusader. I take it that every oil farm that developed an orderly, sober, pleasant community life owed it to a few women who, taking hold from the start, insisted what they considered corrupting influences be cast out. Ida Tarbell's achievements included articles in national magazines and the authorship of several books including the *History of Standard Oil*.

The era of the Civil War called upon women to keep farms, homes, and families intact while men went off to fight. One Rockland Township woman's story is particularly poignant—her drafted husband was forced to leave her alone with four young children, animals to feed, crops to be harvested, and no one to help.

*Office of
The Seneca Kicker.
(left to right)
Anna Kinney,
Anna Hart,
Lucy Williams and
Effie Heckathorn*

Women had little say in the court system of the 1880s, but young Suzanne Beatty nevertheless became a clerk in a Franklin law office, learning all she could about becoming an attorney. Suzanne was so successful that she was admitted to the bar as one of the first women attorneys in Allegheny County.

Venango County women were successful in 1915 in stirring the conscience of voters about the need to permit women to vote. The women's suffrage issue was on the ballot in Pennsylvania that year, and Venango County gave the amendment a 2,007 plurality. While many rural areas voted favorably, the state bowed to a large Philadelphia vote of eight-to-one against the proposal. County newspapers had supported the issue, with the weekly feminist newspaper, *The Seneca Kicker* leading the charge. *The Kicker* advocated "suffrage gardens," ablaze with yellow flowers, and rallies with national speakers. Editor Anna Kinney outdid her daily counterparts in informing the public about the suffrage issue.

For two centuries, Venango County women have met the many and diverse challenges of their generation—hosting quilting bees in their rural farm homes, organizing soup kitchens during the Great Depression, and running machines in factories during the two World Wars—in all they did, striving for a better community.

— CAROLEE MICHENER

Log Cabin/
Straight Furrow
c. 1905
76 x 64 inches
Katherine Liebrich Kugler
(1848–1923)

WHEN LOG CABIN QUILTS REACHED A PEAK OF POPULARITY IN THE LAST QUARTER OF THE nineteenth century, most were made of cottons and wools. Katherine Liebrich Kugler preferred a more elegant look and selected silks for her Log Cabin pattern. She collected many of the fabrics through the years, including silk left from the dress she wore at her wedding. Katherine was of Pennsylvania German heritage; she was born in 1848 in Reading. She married Kasper Kugler, a tool-maker of German heritage born in Belgium. After their marriage they settled in Oil City where Kasper became a member of the city council in 1879. Katherine and Kasper were the parents of six children, whom they reared with the doctrine of Methodism. Katherine made her exceptional Log Cabin quilt c. 1905 in the traditional manner with a red center in each "cabin," signifying the hearth of the home. The diagonal treatment of lights and darks is said to represent the happy and sad times of life.

Katherine Liebrich Kugler

Star of Bethlehem
1939
88 x 88 inches
Stella Collingwood
(—c. 1966)

STELLA COLLINGWOOD BEGAN SEWING THIS STAR OF BETHLEHEM QUILT IN 1938 FOR HER HUSBAND, Henry C. Collingwood. They were living in Bullion when Stella completed the quilt in 1939, and he used it faithfully for a year. Henry was self-employed as an oilman, and in 1940 he was killed when caught in a gasoline engine. Family historians have said that Stella put the quilt away at the time of Henry's death and never used it again. Stella was Henry's second wife, as his first wife died leaving him with one son, Harry Earl. Stella and Henry never had children together, and when she died she passed on the quilt to her stepson, Harry Earl. His son, David Collingwood, now owns the quilt.

Henry C. Collingwood and Stella Collingwood

Whig's Defeat
c. 1865
80 x 78 inches
Rachel Long Ross
(1845–1937)

RACHEL LONG ROSS MADE THIS VARIATION OF WHIG'S DEFEAT C. 1865, WHEN THE WHIGS had been defunct for about ten years. Associations with the Whigs may not have entered Rachel's mind, however, as she was a young bride with at least one child at the time. She married the dapper John P. Ross at about the time the Civil War broke out, 1862, before he left for the war. She may well have made the quilt during the quiet times she had while contemplating his return. After he came home, she was so busy with a growing family that ultimately numbered seven sons and four daughters that she may have forgotten about the Whigs and even making quilts at all. The family attended the Congress Hill Church of God in Sandy Creek, where Rachel is buried. Rachel's mother, Frances Morrison Long, taught her daughter to piece and quilt. They may have worked together on this lovely green and red specimen. Frances was a charter member of the Cranberry Cumberland Presbyterian Church, joining in 1837. Rachel's life spanned eight-seven years, from her birth in Salem in 1845 to her death in Franklin in 1937. Her great-great-granddaughter, Elissa M. Stuttler, Esq., now owns the quilt.

Double Wedding Ring
(pictured)
c. 1935
89 x 82 inches
Zella Cassatt Miller
(1907–)

Double Wedding Ring
c. 1935
88 x 72 inches
Anna Mary Cassatt
Brandon Rembold
(1901–1990)

ZELLA CASSATT AND ANNA MARY CASSATT WERE SISTERS WITH DUTCH ANCESTRY. IN 1935 they together purchased the fabric that they cut, pieced, and quilted with one another. Both young women had already been married and both had young children, so their choice of the Double Wedding Ring pattern may seem surprising; perhaps they just liked it. Anna's husband had died, and the young mothers may have thought a quilting project would take Anna's mind from her grief. She was living with her in-laws, and Zella remembers that Anna's mother-in-law chastised her for wasting thread. The Cassatt girls were born in Clarington and lived in Cranberry and Clarion as adults. There were ten children in the family—five girls and five boys. Cassatt is a familiar name in the world of art, and yes, there is a family connection with the American Impressionist artist Mary Cassatt. The Cassatt sisters were second cousins to Mary, as her father and Anna and Zella's grandfather were brothers. Claiming the pallet they used for the quilts was influenced by cousin Mary might be fun, but the most we can say is that family members generally showed an artistic bent. Anna was six years older than Zella; she died in 1990 at age eighty-nine. Zella will become a nonagenerian on November 7, 1997. She still owns her quilt, and Anna's quilt now belongs to her daughter-in-law Marilyn Craig Brandon. The quilts represent happy memories of times spent together by sisters who chose one another as friends.

Zella Cassatt Miller (left) and Anna Mary Cassatt Brandon Rembold

Nellie Kline Best (left),
Mary Felmlee Best,
and Lester Best,
1950

Mary Olive Best
and Eugene Best,
1940

EUGENE BEST WAS NATURALLY ADEPT AT NEEDLEWORK SINCE BOTH HIS GRANDMOTHER Mary Felmlee Best and mother, Nellie Kline Best, were avid quiltmakers. Eugene and his sister, Mary Olive, were put to work embroidering bears for the quilt by the Best foremothers. While listening to favorite evening radio programs on the battery-operated machine, children also worked on quilts. Eugene says the stitches had to be done properly, as Grandmother Mary Best might make the children rip them out and do them over again. The two families resided in the same house, so Mary and Nellie Best worked together to stitch the squares into a top; they then quilted it. Eugene's Embroidered Bear quilt was made c. 1936, when he was about ten years old, and he remembers that Mary Olive had her own quilt as well. Though Nellie made a different quilt for each family member, Eugene says her specialty was the Double Wedding Ring—made to give to children and grandchildren as wedding gifts. The Best women were members of the Cross Roads Quilting Group near Nickelville (Emlenton), where Eugene and his bears still live. When he married Donna Beels in 1953, the Embroidered Bear quilt was one of their wedding gifts along with one of Nellie's famous Double Wedding Ring quilts.

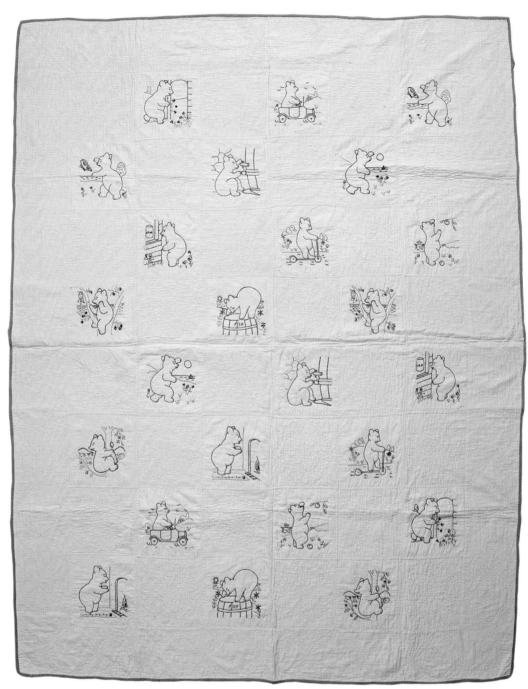

Embroidered Bear
c. 1936
76 x 60 inches
Mary Felmlee Best (1865–1957), Nellie Kline Best
(1894–1988), Mary Olive Best (1925–), and Eugene
Best (1927–)

Warren & Forest Counties

*W*ithin the tapestry of Warren County history are woven the threads of conflict and community. The early history of this area often was one of discord, as the Seneca Nation, with France, England and later, the United States, struggled for control of the land. During the nineteenth century, Yankee settlers arrived to create new communities. With these communities came houses, farms, schools, businesses, and industries, the effects of many of them still visible in the landscape today.

By the sixteenth century the Seneca, members of the Iroquois Nation, controlled the area that is now Warren County. In the eighteenth century, the most noted Seneca was the famous Cornplanter, son of a Dutch trader from Albany and a Seneca mother. After fighting for the British during the Revolution, Cornplanter switched his allegiance and became a defender of the new American government. Following the American Revolution, the new United States secured much of the Seneca homeland through treaties.

In 1795, the town of Warren—named for American patriot Gen. Joseph Warren, killed in the battle of Bunker or Breed's Hill—was laid out by a surveying team led by Gen. William Irvine and Andrew Ellicott. The county, 902 square miles in area, established out of Lycoming and Allegheny Counties by legislation in 1800, is bordered on the north by New York State, on the east by McKean County, on the west by Crawford and Erie Counties, and on the south by Venango and Forest Counties. With few exceptions, the earliest settlers of Warren were Scotch-Irish from southeastern Pennsylvania and New Englanders. Successive waves of immigrants arrived from Germany, Sweden, and Italy during the remaining years of the nineteenth century.

Determining how many of the earliest settlers were women is difficult because their names remain largely unrecorded in early county census, land, and tax records. Many settlers apparently came in family groups because their best chance of survival and success depended on the labor provided by all family members. Originally, hardwood forest covered much of the western portion of the county, while large stands of pine and hemlock grew in the creek valleys and southeast of the Allegheny River. The river and its three major tributaries in Warren County—the Conewango, Brokenstraw, and Kinzua Creeks—were natural waterways for the rafting of lumber, which was the county's main industry for many years. Sawing and rafting of lumber continued into the 1800s.

As the rafting of lumber declined and the arable land was cleared of timber, farming began to flourish, particularly in the northwest section of the county. In addition, the manufacture of furniture and other wood products expanded; the availability of hemlock bark led to the establishment of a large tanning operation in the Sheffield area; and the fabrication of products from iron began its steady climb. The Sunbury and Erie Railroad was completed from Erie to Warren in 1859, greatly facilitating transportation, and by 1883 Warren had become the hub of a network of railroads leading in all directions.

Concurrent with the arrival of the railroad in Warren, oil was discovered at Titusville. In a short time, an oil boom added another major industry, and by the early 1900s thirteen refineries operated within a six-mile radius of Warren. Sensational oil finds occurred in locations including Tidioute, Cherry Grove, and Clarendon. Oil production and refining still are important to the economy of the county.

Through much of the nineteenth century and early twentieth century, the prevailing ideology discouraged or prevented women from fully participating in the business, industry, and politics of the county. Women were urged to focus their energies on home, family, and religion. Many women were charter members of Warren's first churches. Women participated in and led fund-raising activities to pay for constructing churches, and many were members of charitable religious organizations with names such as the Woman's Essential Brigade, The Young Ladies Missionary Society, and The Female Benevolent Society. Many used church quilting bees not only as social occasions but also as opportunities to create products that could be sold or raffled as fund-raisers.

Warren County women often played important roles, both traditional and nontraditional, during the nation's wars. During the Civil War, the Soldiers Aid Society kept women busy making uniforms for the first two companies that left Warren, filling boxes with provisions and clothing for the sick and wounded in hospitals and raising money to provide relief to soldiers and their families. In the wars that followed, similar county organizations, largely founded and staffed by women, continued to provide important services. Many women created quilts with patriotic or commemorative images during wartime. These quilts may have been used in fund-raising activities or kept as personal mementos of an event or loved one.

The second half of the nineteenth century and the early part of the twentieth century witnessed women throughout the United States participating in the club movement. Middle-class Warren women were no exception in striving to form friendships and improve both themselves and their communities through clubs. The Woman's Club, the Garden Club, the Art Club, the Bluestocking Club, the Study Club, and the Chautauqua Literary and Scientific Circle were just a few of those that women organized and joined during this time.

FOREST COUNTY did not exist as a separate entity until 1848, when Jefferson County gave up some of its land; in 1866 a part of Venango was annexed, and Forest was configured as it is today. The original Americans in the area were the Munsee (Delaware), but European occupation began as early as 1749, when Frenchmen visited the western section of the county. David Zeisberger also came to convert the natives and refugees, building his Moravian church in Tionesta in 1769.

The Valentine family settled Jamieson's Flats c. 1797; thereafter arrived Eli Holeman, who operated a ferry business across the Allegheny in 1800; John Middleton, the first teacher, 1802; Poland Hunter in 1805; and others. The first major landholder was Lt. John Range Sr., a Revolutionary War officer whose monument is in the courthouse in Tionesta; he settled in the area in 1815–16.

The first town—Marienville—became the first county seat. Cyrus Blood, a surveyor and educator, built a frame home there in 1843 and called the town Marienville, for his daughter. Court was held in Marienville until 1866 when the borough of Tionesta became the next and present county seat. The early settlers were thrifty, and when the county seat moved, so did the county courthouse. The early frame structure, erected in 1848, was "put on ox wagons and hauled across the county" to Tionesta. It was left even after the brick structure was erected in 1869 but was torn down in the twentieth century. Tionesta, after the creek bearing its name, is a Native-American word meaning, "it penetrates the land."

The area is known for its vast timberlands, and lumbering was an important early industry in the county. The Cook family was instrumental in the timber business and later in preservation of the forest. John Cook, the founder of Cooksburg, settled in the Clarion River Valley in 1825–26, building a log house and sawmill. He had several wives in succession who provided him a strong work force of seventeen children. It was the inspiration of his grandson, Anthony W., to save the forest in 1910, and after much effort in convincing the Pennsylvania legislature, the Cook Forest Association was founded in 1923. Cook Forest State Park emerged as a direct result of his endeavors.

As women demanded and received greater rights in the twentieth century, Warren and Forest County women found new economic and political opportunities. The central role that needlework, and in particular quilting, had played in women's personal, social, and economic activities began to diminish. Quilting, however, still thrives today in both counties, particularly in the cold winter months, and the county's earlier quilts still have the power to evoke memories and delight.

– EDITH SERKOWNEK & CHASE PUTNAM

Crazy Quilt
1918
62 x 45½ inches
Henrietta Ekas

HENRIETTA EKAS OF SHEFFIELD (SOUTHEAST OF WARREN) BECAME A NONAGENERIAN PLUS TWO.
Earlier in Henrietta's life, she celebrated the end of World War I by making
this Crazy Quilt. Both her sons, Miller and Claude Ekas, and her son-in-law,
Claude Landers, fought in the war so it was natural that Henrietta was
happy when the Armistice was signed on November 11, 1918. She included
their names and military insignias as well as the dates of the beginning and
end of the war. Donated by her granddaughter, Virginia Eberhardt, this lap-
sized quilt is from the Collections of the Warren County Historical Society.

*Elizabeth McConnell
Thomas Taylor*

WHITE-ON-WHITE QUILTS OFTEN WERE MADE FOR WEDDINGS. THIS ONE MAY HAVE BEEN started for that occasion, but the date stitched into it, 1853, indicates it was not finished in time for the September 11, 1849, marriage of Elizabeth McConnell Thomas and John Jay Taylor in Conewango Township. The married name of its maker, E. M. Taylor, is also evident. Elizabeth and her sisters and brothers were the children of William Thomas and Jane McConnell Thomas, both born at the turn of the nineteenth century in Schenectady County, New York. Elizabeth was born February 13, 1829, and was only four years old when the family decided to relocate. They rode west on a packet boat via the Erie Canal to Buffalo, and from there hired a team to transport them and their furniture to Farmington, Pennsylvania, where several Schenectady families awaited their arrival. After about three weeks, William continued into Warren County with a friend and bought a four-hundred-acre farm with log cabin on Jackson Run Road in Conewango Township. There Elizabeth and her nine brothers and sisters were reared. Although Elizabeth's White-on-White quilt and her sister Margret Jane Thomas Danforth's Friendship quilt are the only extant Thomas quilts, other family members likely quilted as well. Elizabeth's husband, John Jay, was a businessman active in church and temperance work. Only one daughter, Jennie, survived to adulthood. When she married at her parents' "large, well-furnished home" at the corner of East Street and Fifth Avenue in Warren, Alice Bentley of Meadville (see page 24) was one of the honored guests. After John Jay died in 1899, Elizabeth made her home with Jennie and her husband, H. L. Simpson. When Jennie died in 1909, Elizabeth went to live with sister Margret (whom she called Maggie), then with two of her nieces, one of whom was a nurse. The eighty-five-year-old quiltmaker was revered by her family, who cared for her until her death in 1915. Martha Hill Eaton, one of "Aunt Lib's" great-grandnieces, now owns the quilt.

White-on-White
1853
81 x 76 inches
Elizabeth McConnell Thomas Taylor (1829–1915)

Log Cabin/
Light and Dark
c. 1885
36 x 29 inches
Louisa Paulina Lunn
(1828–1920)

SCANDINAVIAN IMMIGRANTS INTRODUCED THE LOG CABIN TO THE UNITED STATES, AND Louisa Paulina Lunn, a native of Walda Socken, Hallands, Sweden, made this small cradle quilt in the Log Cabin pattern c. 1885. After her eight children were grown, Louisa found the time to stitch the quilt for her granddaughter, Mabel Louise Heald. Louisa's husband, Charles John Lunn, was from the same area of Sweden, and they were married there. He became a cigar-maker after their move to Warren. The Lunns were prolific in their production of babies, with females taking precedence; they had three boys and five girls. Louisa lived to be a nonagenarian, missing her ninety-second birthday by only three weeks. The quilt is now owned by Louisa's great-granddaughter Elaine Louise Heald.

Louisa Paulina Lunn (front row, right)

Crazy Throw
1886–87
56 x 56 inches
Ida Mae Walter

IDA MAE WALTER MADE THIS CRAZY THROW DURING THE WINTER OF 1886–87, WHEN SHE WAS
sixteen years old. Ida was born, raised, and married in Newmansville.
She made the quilt when she was sick; we know that because the letters she embroidered on each tab in her border are strung together
with this message: "Ida Walter was sixteen at time of construction. She
was sick and spent her time sewing." Ida recovered, and ten years later,
on October 19, 1896, she married George B. McKown. They became
the parents of one daughter, Zora, and four sons, Walter, Hobson,
Sherman, and Glenn. In 1916 the family moved to Tidioute where
Zora, Ida's only surviving child, still lives. The ninety-one-year-young
Zora McKown Carnahan now owns the quilt.

Ida Mae Walter McKown

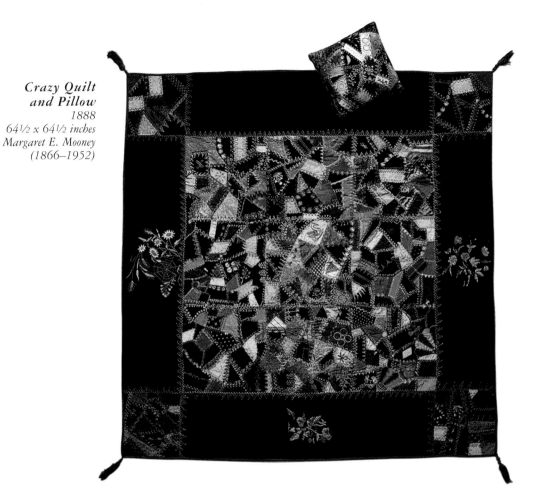

*Crazy Quilt
and Pillow*
1888
64½ x 64½ inches
Margaret E. Mooney
(1866–1952)

Margaret E. Mooney

MARGARET E. MOONEY EARNED HER LIVING AS A SEAMSTRESS. SHE WAS A SPINSTER WHO CLAIMED she died of a broken heart, but she lived until November 17, 1952, sixty-four years after she was "jilted" by her fiancé. Margaret made this exquisite Crazy Quilt and matching pillow for her dowry; the quilt is dated 1888. Family members believe Margaret also embroidered the initials M.E.G., those of her now-long-forgotten fiancé, into the quilt. Margaret's parents, Julia C. Donahue and Roger Mooney, were emigrants from Ireland. Roger and his brother, Thomas, worked in the local tannery. Oil was discovered on the property the brothers bought on Stone Hill in Mead Township, and the family then moved to Warren. The Mooneys seem to have been well-respected as Roger was elected a county commissioner in 1890. At the time of Margaret's death her only sister, Mary A. Mooney, was still living. The quilt and pillow now belong to John and Louise Mangus. John is the son of Helen Mooney Mangus, a cousin of Margaret E. Mooney.

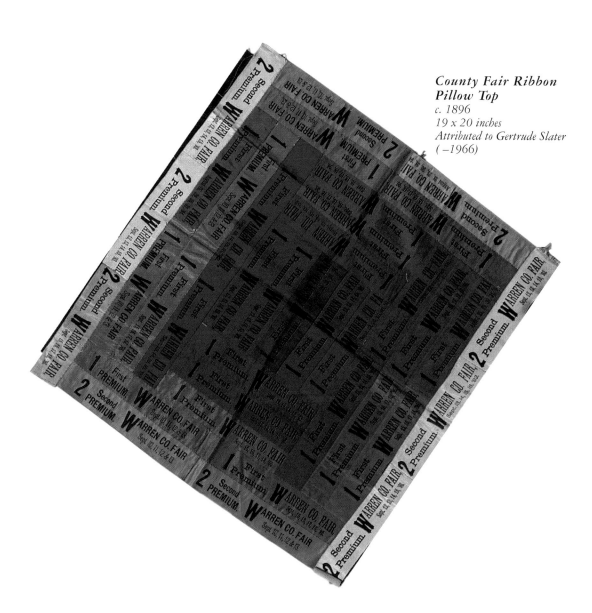

County Fair Ribbon
Pillow Top
c. 1896
19 x 20 inches
Attributed to Gertrude Slater
(–1966)

THE CREATOR OF THIS PILLOW TOP, POSSIBLY GERTRUDE SLATER, MAY HAVE UNDERSTOOD THE
importance of social, cultural, and political roles played by the county fair at
the time she stitched together first- and second-place Warren County Fair
ribbons to make this pillow top. The ribbons she used were from 1892,
1893, 1894, and 1896. Whether Gertrude won them herself is not known,
but in collecting and preserving them she left an important historical document. A lifelong resident of Warren, she died in 1966. The pillow top is
from the Collections of the Warren County Historical Society.

Signature/Fund-raising Quilts

"Sign on the line" became a standard call to action when signature or autograph quilts reached the height of their popularity between 1850 and 1930. Some were made as objects for fund-raising, whereas others commemorated activities or events. Signature quilts evolved as an outgrowth of Friendship and/or Album quilts.

Friendship/Album quilts were made by friends and/or relatives for friends and/or relatives and were often given to an individual who was ill, moving away, or celebrating a special event. A change occurred with Signature/Fund-raising quilts when individuals who wanted the opportunity to sign a block for inclusion in a quilt were required to donate a specified sum of money—usually a dime, but occasionally twenty-five to fifty cents. In addition to the funds generated through name-signing, the quilts were sometimes auctioned or "chanced off." Raffle tickets were used before the 1890s, but when members of the Women's Christian Temperance Union (WCTU) linked gambling to drink, raffling declined. The December 1917 issue of *The Modern Priscilla*, illustrated a "ticket form" that readers could copy when selling name designations in making Red Cross quilts.

Quilt historian Dorothy Cozart has linked the beginnings of fund-raising quilts with the antislavery movement. She located an 1837 cradle quilt among the collections of the Society for the Preservation of Antiquities that was sold at an antislavery fair in Boston. The War Between the States provided the impetus for an epidemic of quiltmaking. Northern women made quilts and comforts for Union soldiers and hospital beds. Although northern "Sanitary Fairs" were devoted to fund-raising, not one specific Sanitary Fair quilt has been found; perhaps the women were too busy organizing the fairs. In the South, embargoes made cloth scarce, but some southern women managed to piece and quilt to raise money for Confederate efforts. Quilt historians have found evidence of two quilts auctioned on subsequent occasions, thus providing additional funds for the soldiers each time the auctioneer's gavel resounded. Though these particular quilts were definitely conceived with fund-raising in mind, no signatures were affixed to them. Fund-raising has no hard, fast rules; signatures were often a vehicle to raise money, but auctioning and raffling quilts without names were viable methods, too. And some signature quilts have nothing to do with raising funds.

In the nineteenth century, fund-raising quilts increased in popularity with the advance of the women's club movement and the accessibility of printed patterns in such magazines as *Peterson's*, *Arthur's*, *The American Agriculturalist*, *Good Housekeeping*, and *The National Stockman and Farmer*. Often the quilts were made in concert with the need for a new church; churchwomen's organizations, often known as the Ladies Aid Society, could raise funds to pay for building at least half the church. According to Cozart, Methodist women seldom raised more than three hundred dollars with a quilt, but construction of a church of the 1890s might cost around just seven hundred dollars. Crazy Quilts do not often appear to have fund-raising connections, but more may have been used for the purpose than some historians realize. After a decline in the late nineteenth century, fund-raising quilts rose in popularity again when women rallied to provide goods and services for the soldiers of World War I. This time southern and northern women joined together in the effort that centered in the American Red Cross.

The signature quilts encountered during the documentation phase of this project are "wonderfully varied," according to Jeannette Lasansky. This may be a consequence of the Pennsylvania origins of fund-raising signature quilts that Cozart identified in her 1988 paper, "The Role and Look of Fundraising Quilts, 1850-1930." Because they were identified as one of the strengths of our documentation phase and since we wanted to weave all of the counties together in a final statement, we feature in this last chapter one signature quilt from each county. Every quilt may not have served a fund-raising function, but together these quilts represent a group effort for reasons in addition to friendship.

The WCTU and the Methodist Church played a prominent role in fund-raising signature quilts. The connection between the two groups may be a natural outgrowth of WCTU founder Frances Willard's membership in, and preference for, the Methodist denomination of the Protestant church. Our WCTU Crusade quilt (page 78) was made in Clarion County in 1934, apparently for the sixtieth anniversary of the local chapter. In a poignant way, the quilt stands as a testimony to the anonymity of women in American *his*tory, as little information about the Clarion WCTU and the women who made the quilt is available. Perhaps because they were donated to historical societies, a bit more is known about the McKean Red Cross quilt (page 85) and the Warren County Centennial quilt (page 81). The Red Cross quilt was made as a fund-raiser; on the back of the quilt a gentleman recorded the amount of money that was raised through it. The McKean Chapter of the American Red Cross solicited money for signatures in many corners of northwest Pennsylvania. Sharon is approximately seventy miles from McKean, and the group received a donation from the teachers there. A business from nearby Edinboro contributed, as did NuBone Corset, then in Corry, and Erie's Atlantic Refining Company. One eye doctor saw the quilt as an advertisement and had a pair of spectacles stitched into it. Let's hope his investment paid off!

The names of no businesses adorn the Warren Centennial Quilt, but twenty-nine women's names are featured. Though this textile document was given to the historical society in 1968, whether the women made it with friendship or fund-raising in mind is not known. We are also unsure as to whether the Keystone Grange quilt (page 83) was made as a fund-raiser, but with twenty-six signed blocks each containing about twenty names, it likely was used for that purpose. If only the people who signed their names had known the questions we might ask!

Methodists figured prominently in our study of fund-raising signature quilts, as they have nationwide. The women of the Reno Methodist Episcopal Church made their quilt sometime between 1865, when the church was founded, and 1872, when the Woman's Foreign Missionary Society was organized (as the first chapter in the Erie Conference). Whether folks paid to have their signatures included is unclear; but once completed, the quilt *was* "chanced off." A similar situation seems to have occurred years later (1935) at the White Chapel Methodist Episcopal Church in New Wilmington, Mercer County. The signatures on the quilt made by the Missionary Society (page 87) had to be purchased for ten cents each, and when it was completed, the quilt was sold to the highest bidder. By this time, the fund-raising capabilities of the signature quilt were beginning to wane, and the seventy-five dollars reportedly earned by the group did not compare with the hundreds of dollars nineteenth-century women had collected. By the time of the World War II, many women had gone to work in factories, and fund-raising signature quilts were practically a thing of the past.

— M A R I A N N E   B E R G E R   W O O D S

Signature
1934
88 x 79 inches
Clarion Women's
Christian Temperance Union
"Crusade quilt"

THE WOMEN'S CHRISTIAN TEMPERANCE UNION (WCTU) WAS IMPORTANT TO MANY WOMEN living in the eastern and midwestern sections of America in the late-nineteenth/early-twentieth centuries. Clarion was one city whose female residents took part in this crusade against drink. The WCTU Crusade Signature quilt was made in 1934, possibly to celebrate the sixtieth anniversary of the local chapter. The quilt's inscription states, "Crusade quilt, Clarion WCTU, 1874–1934." The January 11, 1934, issue of the *Clarion Republican* noted there would be an all-day meeting of the "Union" at the Methodist Episcopal Church on January 17, "New Crusade Day." The report continued: "The Union is planning on beginning the Crusade quilt. If the quilt is begun on that day it will be [a] significant memento of the new crusade." So, though the quilt had more to do with "New Crusade Day" than the sixtieth anniversary, the specific dates on the quilt furnish an unsolved mystery. In May 1934 the quilt, with names arranged in a star configuration, was completed. The *Republican* mentioned that the crusade quilt was "on exhibition and [is] very much admired by all." Yvonne Haskell now owns the quilt.

Signature
c. 1865–72
86 x 66 inches
Members of the Reno
Methodist Episcopal Church
Venango County

ALMOST A CENTURY BEFORE DONALD L. WILSON AND LINDA L. YOUNG WERE WED IN 1963, this Signature quilt was destined for their home. Donald's great-grandparents Edward and Wilhamena McDowell obtained the quilt from a sale at the Reno Methodist Episcopal Church so as to pass down to the first-born of each generation at the time of his marriage (there has been a son in each generation thus far). Robert Y. Wilson and Elsie McDowell first received it when they married in 1908. Elsie, who lived to be one week shy of 101, gave the quilt to her son Frank upon his marriage to Christina in 1943. Apparently Frank and Christina did not produce the first child of the next generation, as nephew Donald and his wife, Linda, next received the quilt. When their son, Steven Scott Wilson, marries, Steven and his wife will receive it. The signatures are embroidered in red in a block motif with diagonal intersections. The history of the quilt has taken a back seat to its lineage; but since the Methodists were adept at the "business" of quiltmaking, we believe it was a fund-raiser. The McDowell family were early settlers of Venango County with the arrival of Colonel McDowell and his wife, Sarah, in 1794 (see page 54).

Elsie McDowell Wilson

The Centennial Quilting Party, 1895

WHEN WARREN CITY CELEBRATED ITS CENTENNIAL IN 1895, THE WOMEN GOT TOGETHER to construct this Signature quilt. Tamar Gilbert Rockwell may have conceived the idea as the quilt remained in the Rockwell family for a long time, but, it was ultimately given to the Warren County Historical Society by Mrs. Robert Trusler. Near the center is found the inscription, "1795 Warren Centennial 1895." The quilt seems to be more commemorative than fund-raising in intent. Twenty-nine women signed the quilt, and a few noted their octagenarian status alongside their names.
The signers were:

Catherine Alden   Josephine E. Mease
Maria C. Allen   Jane E. Merrill
Sahra E. Allen   Rose Gemmill Messner
Matilda L. Ball   Arabella W. Parshall
Nellie S. Beaty   Martha W. Pierce
Mary E. Bemis   Tamar Gilbert Rockwell
Jennie Stranahan Brecht   Jessie Dunham Stewart
Susan T. Daggett   Sarah Ann Sturgeon 86 years
Salome Arnette Galligan   Hattie M. Talbott
Mary P. Gerould   Charlotte L. Waters
Clarissa Gilbert 82 years   Rosamond Hall Waters
Isabel Weatherly Henry   Rachel Weatherby 87 years
May Rockwell Henry   D. H. White 82 years
Nancy L. Hoffman   Florence S. Wood
Sahra Antoinette King

Signature
1895
85 x76 inches
Warren Centennial

WHEN MEMBERS OF THE KEYSTONE GRANGE GOT TOGETHER TO STITCH THIS SIGNATURE quilt in 1909, the Grange movement had been in existence for more than forty years. Oliver Hudson Kelley founded the national Grange, officially known as the Patrons of Husbandry, in 1867, to support farmers and farm issues. This embroidered quilt has a variety of designs and a nice touch of floral sprays in each corner. The sheaf of wheat, shown on one of the quilt blocks, had special meaning for the Patrons of Husbandry. In 1988, Charles E. Wismer, Pennsylvania State Grange Master, said in a visit to the Hayfield Grange (into which the Keystone Grange was absorbed):

> A successful grange is like a sheaf of wheat. It's beautiful when all the heads and stalks are twined together. The twine is the state grange, the stalks are the local granges, the heads are the subordinate granges, and the granges within the heads are the grange members, If you are all together, working properly, you have a beautiful organization.

Given its preponderance of local names, the quilt likely was made as a fund-raiser. Near its center, the words "Keystone Grange" are embroidered with the number "901" and "P of H" (Patrons of Husbandry) in a modified keystone configuration. The words "Hettie Graham, Lloy[d] Graham, Master, '09" are embroidered below. Another block lists masters of the organization with their dates of service:

D. H. Lefever, 1890–'91	W. A. Dearborn, 1900–'06
C. H. Lefever, 1892	W. J. Graham, 1901–'03–'04–'05
Helen Johnson, 1893–'99	A. E. Lake, 1902
E. L. Gaut, 1895	Lloyd Graham, 1908–'09
George Johnson, 1896–'97	Addie Yunker, 1910
R. A. Fisk, 1898	

The Keystone Grange was located at Littles Corners, Hayfield Township. The charter was issued on January 11, 1890, and the group disbanded in 1965. Ruth Koehler McMillon, whose husband, Hugh McMillon, signed his name in one of the blocks, gave the quilt to her niece JoAnn Toner for safekeeping in 1986.

Signature
1909—10
79 x 69 inches
Keystone Grange

AT THE OUTBREAK OF WORLD WAR I, MANY BRANCHES OF THE AMERICAN RED CROSS WORKED to produce fund-raising quilts. In December 1917, *The Modern Priscilla* printed a full page of instructions on how to make a quilt, stating, "One thousand dollars for the Red Cross can be raised on a memorial quilt." The McKean Chapter did not rely on the instructions *The Modern Priscilla* provided, however. Though this quilt is clad in red and white as one might imagine each Red Cross quilt to be, it is not at all like the one suggested in the magazine. Nor did the McKean branch make the goal set by the magazine. Each of the forty-two circles represents a donation of one dollar, and each of the fifteen to sixteen spokes comprising each circle cost its donor ten cents. According to the inscription written by Harry E. Steadman on the back, the donations totaled $188.11. The signatures, written in indelible ink, are those of the men, women, and businesses of McKean Township and surrounding area who donated to the cause. They include: NuBone Corset Company (Corry, Pennsylvania) Agent: Emma J. Moore; The Atlantic Refining Co.; McKean Ladies Orchestra, S. S. Blanigen, Director; Prospect Heights Teachers (Sharon, Pennsylvania); N. Kupper Photography; Steadman Brothers; Talmadge & Sterrett, Farm Implements, McKean, Pennsylvania; and Milton Donor General Store. Dr. J. K. Morris, Erie, Pennsylvania, signed his name and included his "spectacle" logo. The Surgical Dressing Class noted that the quilt was signed by "Members Present, Nov. 19, 1918." The twenty-five local men then serving in the U.S. armed forces are listed in the corners. Hugh Trask, who had been taken prisoner, is also listed. At the top of the quilt is a lone star with the name of Levi Sybrandt, a young man who had been killed in action. Five red crosses were stitched into the back. This quilt, constructed in 1918, is from the Collections of the Erie County Historical Society.

Signature/Fund-raiser
c. 1918
87 x 80 inches
McKean Chapter, American Red Cross

*Missionary Society,
White Chapel Methodist
Episcopal Church
(Raimie Canon Cox —
back row, far right,
holding a child)*

IN 1935, THE MISSIONARY SOCIETY OF THE WHITE CHAPEL METHODIST EPISCOPAL CHURCH IN
New Wilmington decided to raise funds by making a quilt. Each person who signed her/his name paid ten cents for the privilege, and the Missionary Society auctioned the quilt after its completion. The group was determined to follow a standard circular format, with sixteen names in each of the twenty-five blocks. But the hot-pink embroidery floss and the hot-pink cotton chosen for the sashing and border were far from common! This Signature/Fund-raiser was signed by its current owner, Catheryn R. Cox Moose, as well as her mother, Raymie Canon Cox, who was one of the Missionary Society women shown in the photograph, taken around the time the quilt was made. The women took time from their embroidery

*White Chapel Methodist
Episcopal Church*

and quilting to have a picnic; naturally, the children were invited, too. When the quilt was auctioned, Raymie wanted it very much, but she had only so much cash available. Pearson Cox, knowing how much his wife wanted the quilt, continued bidding and secured the quilt for thirty-five dollars—then a high price. But Raymie was happy, it was for a good cause, and the Missionary Society was able to help those less fortunate by sending seventy-five dollars to the headquarters of the Methodist Church.

Signature/Fund-raiser
1935
80 x 80 inches
Missionary Society, White Chapel Methodist Episcopal
Church, New Wilmington

Bibliography

Quilt Bibliography

Benberry, Cuesta. "The 20th Century's First Quilt Revival. Part III: The World War I Era," *Quilter's Newsletter Magazine* (October 1979: 10–11, 29.

Binney, Edwin III, and Gail Binney-Winslow. *Homage to Amanda: Two Hundred Years of American Quilts*. San Francisco: R K Press, 1984.

Bishop, Robert, and Carter Houck. *All Flags Flying: American Patriotic Quilts as Expressions of Liberty*. New York: E. P. Dutton, 1986.
———. *Quilts, Coverlets, Rugs & Samplers*. New York: Chanticleer, 1982.

Bowman, Doris M. *The Smithsonian Treasury: American Quilts*. Washington, D.C.: Smithsonian Institution, 1991.

Clark, Ricky. *Quilted Gardens: Floral Quilts of the Nineteenth Century*. Nashville: Rutledge Hill Press, 1994.
———, ed. *Quilts in Community: Ohio's Traditions*. Nashville: Rutledge Hill Press, 1991.
———, et al. *Quilts and Carousels: Folk Art in the Firelands*. Oberlin, Ohio: Firelands Center for the Visual Arts, 1983.

Cozart, Dorothy. "The Role and Look of Fundraising Quilts: 1850–1930." *Pieced by Mother: Symposium Papers*. Lewisburg, Pennsylvania: Union County Historical Society, 1988, pp. 86–95.

Cooper, Patricia, and Norma Bradley Buferd. *The Quilters: Women and Domestic Art, An Oral History*. Garden City, New Jersey: Anchor/Doubleday, 1977.

Ferrero, Pat, Elaine Hedges, and Julie Silber. *Hearts and Hands: The Influence of Women and Quilts on American Society*. San Francisco: Quilt Digest, 1987.

Finley, John. *Kentucky Quilts, 1800–1900*. Louisville, Kentucky: Kentucky Quilt Project, 1982.

Glassie, Henry. *Pattern in the Material Folk Culture of the Eastern United States*. Philadelphia: University of Pennsylvania, 1968.

Gunn, Virginia. *Heart of Pennsylvania: Symposium Papers*. Lewisburg, Pennsylvania: Oral Traditions Project, 1986, pp. 90–95.

Hafter, Daryl M. "Toward a Social History of Needlework Artists." *Woman's Art Journal* 2 (Fall/Winter 1982): 25–29.

Havig, Bettina. *Missouri Heritage Quilts*. Paducah, Kentucky: American Quilter's Society, 1986.

Herr, Patricia T. "What Distinguishes a Pennsylvania Quilt?" *In the Heart of Pennsylvania: Symposium Papers*. Lewisburg, Pennsylvania: Oral Traditions Project, 1986, pp. 28–37.

Hoffman, Lynn T. *Patterns in Time: Quilts of Western New York*. Buffalo, New York: Buffalo and Erie County Historical Society, 1990.

Hollstein, Jonathon. *The Pieced Quilt: An American Design Tradition*. Boston: Little, Brown, 1983.

Horton, Laurel, and Lynn Robertson Myers. *Social Fabric: South Carolina's Traditional Quilts*. McKissick Museum, The University of South Carolina, n.d.

Irwin, John Rice. *A People and Their Quilts*. Exton, Pennsylvania: Schiffer, 1884.

Keller, Patricia J. *'Of the Best Sort but Plain': Quaker Quilts from the Delaware Valley, Chadds Ford*, Pennsylvania: Brandywine River Museum, 1997.

Kiracofe, Roderick, and Mary Elizabeth Johnson. *The American Quilt: A History of Cloth and Comfort, 1750–1950*. New York: Clarkson Potter, 1993.

Lasansky, Jeannette. "Quilts of Central Pennsylvania." *Antiques* 131 no. 1 (January 1987): 288–99.

Lasansky, Jeannette, et al. *Heart of Pennsylvania: Symposium Papers*. Lewisburg, Pennsylvania: Oral Traditions Project, 1986, pp. 90–95.
———. *On the Cutting Edge: Textile Collectors, Collections, and Traditions*. Lewisburg, Pennsylvania: Union County Historical Society, 1994.
———. *Pieced by Mother: Symposium Papers*. Lewisburg, Pennsylvania: Union County Historical Society, 1988.
———. *Pieced by Mother: Over 100 Years of Quiltmaking Traditions*. Lewisburg, Pennsylvania: Union County Historical Society, 1987.

Laury, Jean Ray. *Ho for California: Pioneer Women and Their Quilts*. New York: Dutton, 1990.

Lipsett, Linda Otto. *Remember Me: Women and Their Friendship Quilts*. San Francisco: Quilt Digest, 1985.

Luster, Michael. *Stitches in Time: A Legacy of Ozark Quilts*. Rogers, Arkansas: Rogers Historical Museum, 1986.

Mainardi, Patricia. "Quilts: The Great American Art." *Feminism and Art History*, ed. Norma Broude and Mary D. Garrard. New York: Harper and Row, 1982.

Melvin, Patricia Mooney. *Ohio Quilts and Quilters: 1800–1981*. Wooster, Ohio: College of Wooster, 1981.

Orlofsky, Patsy and Myron. *Quilts in America*. New York: McGraw-Hill, 1974.

Pilgrim, Paul, and Gerald E. Roy. *Gatherings: America's Quilt Heritage*. Paducah, Kentucky: American Quilter's Society, 1995.

Ramsey, Bets, and Merikay Waldvogel. *The Quilts of Tennessee: Images of Domestic Life Prior to 1930*. Nashville, Tennessee: Routledge, 1986.

Rubin, Cynthia Elyce, ed. *Southern Folk Art*. Birmingham, Alabama: Oxmoor House, 1985.

Safford, Carleton L., and Robert Bishop. *America's Quilts and Coverlets*. New York: Bonanza, 1985 ed.

Shaw, Robert. *Quilts: A Living Tradition*. New York: Hough Lauter Levin, 1995.

Shine, Caroline R. *Quilts from Cincinnati Collections*. Cincinnati, Ohio: Cincinnati Art Museum, 1985.

Sullivan, Kathlyn F. *Gatherings: America's Quilt Heritage*. Paducah, Kentucky: American Quilter's Society, 1995.

Torsney, Cheryl B., and Judy Elsley. *Quilt Culture: Tracing the Pattern*. Columbia: University of Missouri, 1994.

Turner, Evan H. *North Carolina Country Quilts: Regional Variations*. Chapel Hill, North Caroline: Ackland Art Museum, 1979.

REGIONAL HISTORY BIBLIOGRAPHY

Anon. Clarion County Centennial. [Clarion, Pennsylvania]: 1940.
———. *Combination Atlas of the County of Mercer and the State of Pennsylvania*. Philadelphia: F. M. Hopkins, 1873.
———. *Combination Atlas Map of Crawford County Pennsylvania*, Philadelphia: Evers, Ensign & Evers,1876.
———. *Grove City Reporter Herald*, August 22, 1938.
———. *The Historical Album*. Franklin, Pennsylvania: 1968.
———. *History of Crawford County, Pennsylvania*.
Evansville, Indiana: Unigraphic, 1975.
———. *History of Mercer County, Pennsylvania*. Chicago: Brown, Runk, 1888.
———. *History of Venango County, Pennsylvania*. Franklin, Pennsylvania: Venango County Historical Society, 1984.
———. *The Lawrence Journal*, March 5, 1854.
———. *Nelson's Biographical Dictionary and Historical Reference Book of Erie County, Pennsylvania*. Erie, Pennsylvania: S. B. Nelson, 1896.

Babcock, C. A. *Venango County, Pennsylvania: Her Pioneers and Her People*. Chicago: 1909.

Bartlett, Virginia K. *Keeping House: Women's Lives in Western Pennsylvania, 1790–1850*. Pittsburgh: Historical Society of Western Pennsylvania and Universtiy of Pittsburgh Press, 1994.

Bates, Samuel Penniman. *Our County and Its People: A Historical and Record of Crawford County, Pennsylvania*. Boston: W.A. Fergusson, 1899.
———, et al. *History Erie County*. Warner, Beers, 1884.

Bell, H. C., ed. *History of Venango County, Pennsylvania*. Chicago: 1890.

Bristow, Arch. *Old Time Tales of Warren County: A Collection of the Picturesque and Romantic Lore of Early Days in Warren County, Pennsylvania*. Meadville, Pennsylvania: Tribune Publishing, 1932.

Brown, R. C., et al. *History of Crawford County, Pennsylvania*. Chicago: 1885.

Caldwell, J. A. *Caldwell's Illustrated Historical Combination Atlas of Clarion County, Pennsylvania*. Condit, Ohio: 1877. Reprint, Rimersburg, Pennsylvania: 1964.

Carney, John G. *Tales of Old Erie*. Erie: Advance Printing and Litho, 1958.

Clark, Mabel K. *Titusville: An Illustrated History*. Cambridge, Maryland: Western Publishing, 1976.

Conn, Mabel K. *Ida Tarbell, Muckraker*. Nashville, New York: Thomas Nelson, 1972.

Davis, A. J. *History of Clarion County, Pennsylvania*. Syracuse, New York: 1887. Reprint, Rimersburg, Pennsylvania: 1968.

Dayton, David M. *'Mid the Pines*. Grove City, Pennsylvania: 1971.

Durant, S. W. *History of Mercer County, Pennsylvania*. Philadelphia, 1877.
———. *History of Mercer County, Pennsylvania*. Chicago: 1888.

Freeman, Sabina Shields, and Margaret L. Tenpas. *Erie History— the Women's Story*. Erie, Pennsylvania: Benet Press for American Association of University Women, 1982.
———. *The Battles Story*. Erie, Pennsylvania: Published by author, 1992.

Gray, Mrs. George. *Interesting History of the North East W.C.T.U. Chapter*. North East, Pennsylvania: Isabel Hall Union, W.C.T.U.: nd.

Harpster, John W., ed. *Pen Pictures of Early Western Pennsylvania*. Pittsburgh: University of Pittsburgh Press, 1938.

Helmreich, Jonathan. *The First 100 Years of Settlement and Growth in Crawford County, Pennsylvania*. Meadville, Pennsylvania: Crawford County Historical Society, 1987.

Huidekoper, Alfred. *Incidents in the Early History of Crawford County*. Philadelphia: 1850.

Hunter, William A. *Forts on the Pennsylvania Frontier, 1753–1758*. Harrisburg, Pennsylvania: Pennsylvnaia Historical and Museum Commission, 1960.

Irwin, S. D. *History of Forest County*. Tionesta, Pennsylvania: 1876.

Jordan, John W. *Genealogical and Personal History of Western Pennsylvania*. New York: Lewis Historical Publishing, 1915.

Leeson, M. A., ed. *History of the Counties of McKean, Elk, Forest, Cameron and Potter, Pennsylvania*. Chicago: 1890.

Marsh, John L., Ph.D. *Edinboro: A Dirt Street Town*. Edinboro, Pennsylvania: Rotary Club, 1976.

Miller, F. G. *Our Own Pioneers*. Meadville, Pennsylvania: 1929.

Miller, John. *A Twentieth Century History of Erie County, Pennsylvania*, 2 vols. Chicago: Lewis Publishing, 1909.

Newton, J. H. *History of Venango County, Pennsylvania*. Columbus, Ohio: 1879.

Putnam, Mary and Chase, eds. *Historic Buildings in Warren County*, 3 vols. [Warren, Pennsylvania]: 1971–74.

Reed, J. E. *History of Erie County, Pennsylvania*. Indianapolis, Indiana: 1925.

Reynolds, J. E. *In French Creek Valley*. Meadville, Pennsylvania: 1938.

Robbins, D. P. *Popular History of Erie County,* Pennsylvania. Philadelphia, 1894.

Sanford, Laura G. *History of Erie County, Pennsylvania* (rev. ed.). Philadelphia: J. B. Lippincot, 1894.

Schenck, J. S., ed. *History of Warren County, Pennsylvania*. Syracuse, New York, 1887.

Schoolcraft, Henry R. *Information Respecting the History Condition and Prospects of the Indian Tribes of the United States, Part IV and V*. Philadelphia: J. B. Lippincott, 1855.

Smeltzer, Wallace Guy. *The History of United Methodism in Western Pennsylvania*. Nashville, Tennessee: Parthenon, 1975.

Smith, B. A., ed. *Historical Collections of Sheffield Township. Warren County, Pennsylvania*. Warren, Pennsylvania: 1943.

Spencer, Herbert Reynolds. *Erie . . . A History*. Erie, Pennsylvania: n.p., 1962.
——— and Walter Jack. *Roaming Erie County Pennsylvania*. Erie, Pennsylvania: 1958.

Stewart, Anne W. *A Concise History of the City of Meadville*. 1993.

Swetnam, George, and Helene Smith. *A Guidebook to Historic Western Pennsylvania*. Pittsburgh: University of Pittsburgh, 1976.

Tarbell, Ida. "Diamond Jubilee Celebration Paper." Titusville, Pennsylvania: Drake Well Museum: 1934.
———. *All in the Day's Work: An Autobiography*. New York: Macmillan, 1939.
———. *The History of the Standard Oil Company*. 2 vols. Glouster, Massachusetts: Peter Smith, 1963.

Thomas, Elisha. "Reminiscences of Early Life." ***Stepping Stones***. Warren, Pennsylvania: Warren County Historica Society, n.d.

Vance, Russell E., Jr. *A Portrait of Edinboro from Private Academy to State College, 1856–1976*. Rochester, New York: PSI, 1977.

Wellejus, Edward. *Chronicle of a Great Lakes City*. Woodland Hills, California: Windsor, 1980.

White, J. G., ed. *A 20th Century History of Mercer County, Pennsylvania*. New York: n.p., 1909.

Whitman, Benjamin and Russell, N. W. *History of Erie County, Pennsylvania*. Chicago: 1884.

Wilbur, Earl Morse. *A Historical Sketch of the Independent Congregational Church, Meadville, Pennsylvania, 1825–1900*. Meadville, Pennsylvania: n.p., 1902.

Quilt Discovery Day Volunteers

CLARION COUNTY

Chairs: Carol Kennemuth and Janice Horn
Helpers: Peggy Allison, Cherie Baronowski, Paula Bowersox, Sally Byers, Margaret Buckwalter, Jean Chitester, Ann Port Denio, Mary Duncan, Gladys Ferringer, Elisabeth Fulmer, Bernice Gourley, Mary Lou Hetrick, Alice Himes, Marian Kapity, Iseli Krauss, Loretta McNaughton, Grace Miller, Norma Jean Miller, Lois Owen, Faye Park, Yvonne Perches, Mary Jo Rees, Cathy Schrecengost, Dorothy Schwabenbauer, and Joan Smith

CRAWFORD COUNTY

Chairs: Ruth Prest and Nancy Heath
Helpers: Suzanne Adham, Janet Applegate, Gwendolyn Barboni, Miriam Bowman, Ruth Bragg, Marge Curtis, Dorothy Englert, Lynette Fabian, Kate Firer, Bev Gable, Mary Lou Giles, Anne Hall, Becky Hall, Marie Hamilton, Nancy Heath, Gerrie Heibel, Nancy Helmreich, Mike Hyde, Vivian Hyde, Dolores Joshua, Molly Keenan, Marni Kirkpatrick, June Kleeman, Nancy Larko, Annette Lynch, Julia Marshall, Nancy Monnin, Joan Petruso, Ruth Pierson, Sigrid Piroch, Carol Prather, Leslie Przybylek, Edith Rabel, Dolores Reichel, Barbara Saulsbery, Mary Schliecker, Caroline Sherman, Mary Jo Smock, Sophia Spencer, Peg Weymer, Lula Williams, and Photographer, Dick Kleeman

ERIE COUNTY

Chairs: Calla Joy Rose and Susan Beates Hansen
Helpers: Anita Andrick, Carolyn Baxter, Marge Beates, Marilyn Bedford, Dorothy Bennett, Grace Blount, Kay Buffington, Avis Burns, Betty Charters, Margaret Conners, Julie Fera, Pauline Fisher, Lucy Fuller, Ruth Getz, Florance Grice, Judy Heinz, Carol Henderson, Barbara Hutzelman, Nicki Jares, Mary Ann Kallenbach, Peg Krieder, Jutta Krieger, Sara Krieger, Jenny Lanning, Gert Leffingwell, Judy Lyon, Irene Merryman, Christine Mitchell, Donna Lee Morschauser, Jean Nemenz, Beverly Pryor, Jo Rogers, Eleanor Sample, Barbara Seidler, Callie Steckler, Carol Taylor, Dolores Thompson, Barbara Toy, Jackie Viestenz, and Sandy Ward

MERCER COUNTY

Chairs: Jane Clark and Peg Weymer
Helpers: Cindy Beggs, Joan Brandt, Bert Lackey, Judy Ligo, Rhoda McCartney, Janet McDougall, Margaret McDougall, Edith McGhee, Donna Montgomery, Vivian Moon, Janet Runkle, Barbara Shuck, Shirley Staph, Lucille Urmson, Berdella Wimer

VENANGO COUNTY

Chairs: Phyllis Weltner and Rainy Linn
Helpers: Louise Aaron, Ellen Jane Allen, Patricia Best, Marilyn Brandon, Evelyn Burchfield, Sue Chatham, Ruth Edge, Gerald Fisher, Bonnie Harshaw, Ruth Heasley, Katherine Heber, Rachel Hoover, Mary Lou Lazar, Susan Lineman, Jo McCracken, Viola Russell, Sally McKissick, Mary Lou Mook, Viola Russell, Faye J. Smith, Jean Stellman, Elissa M. Stuttler, Barbara Watkins, and Virginia Weltner

WARREN/FOREST COUNTIES

Chairs: Edith Serkownek and Gladys Herrick
Helpers: Evelyn Haller, Dorothy McCarthy, Marsha McKown, Olivia Sechriest, and Judi Wilson

Index